Biblical
Beliefs

Biblical Beliefs

DOCTRINES BELIEVERS SHOULD KNOW

EVANGELICAL TRAINING ASSOCIATION

Unless otherwise noted, Scripture quotations are from The Holy Bible, English Standard Version ®
ESV®, copyright ©2001 by Crossway, a publishing ministry of Good News Publishers. Used by
permission. All rights reserved.

Scripture marked (KJV) is from the King James Version.

Cover design: Urban Ministries, Calumet City, IL

Interior design and typesetting: Larry Taylor Design, Ltd.

ISBN: 978-1-929852-10-9

7 6 5 4 3 2 1 3 2 1 0 9

Contents

Introduction

What was it that led to the early church's success? This certainly does not mean success in its political clout or influence. It cannot mean financial success, for most early Christians were poor. In fact, Christians were largely the victims of verbal, political, and physical persecution for their profession that Jesus Christ was Lord. Yet despite the short-term victories of their enemies, Christianity eventually became the most dominant religious force the world has ever seen. To paraphrase one social commentator on church history, the life of the early church is a story of "how the obscure, marginal Jesus movement became the dominant religious force in the western world in a few centuries."[1]

As many historians have noted, Christianity became influential because of how its message informed its deeds. Christians stood out because they cared for the ill, the marginalized, and the needy.[2] They were, as one of the early apologists argued, good citizens whose manner of life—despite how strange their beliefs were—was helpful for society. Yet it was their fundamental faith commitments that supported that lifestyle. This relationship between beliefs and behavior, or doctrine and practice, is exactly what made all the difference. This is what Christian ministry—and this book—is all about.

The Apostle Paul emphasizes doctrine as a crucial ingredient to the church's health in Ephesians 4. He explains that the entire purpose of Christian ministry is Christian maturity. Throughout the rest of that epistle, Paul then describes how this maturity is cultivated in the church. But before developing this, he notes in chapter four that maturity prevents believers from being "tossed to and fro by the waves and carried about by every wind of doctrine, by human cunning, by craftiness in deceitful schemes" (Ephesians 4:14). In other words, deception is a significant danger for Christians. The truth, then, becomes essential for living in such a perilous time.

In 2003, Dan Brown's book *The Da Vinci Code* rocked the Protestant and

7

Catholic communities. Though it was classified as a novel, many lamented the way it so transparently undermined historic beliefs about the identity of Jesus and the character of the Christian Gospels. Many responded to this popular book in the form of books, pamphlets, and short films designed to discredit Brown's subtle attack on Christianity. Many of the same complaints were logged following the 2007 release of *The Golden Compass,* a film-adaptation of a 1997 novel. In this trilogy, author Phillip Pullman unashamedly attempted to undermine the credibility and authority of the institutional church. Naturally, many Christians protested this film and even staged boycotts. They responded adversely to both *The Da Vinci Code* and *The Golden Compass* because they saw these as attacks on the truth.

Defending the faith in a post-Christian culture is an important task. One of the possible outcomes of those who read and reflect upon this book carefully is that they will be better equipped to contend for the faith, as the book of Jude encourages us to do. However, this task belongs more properly to the discipline known as apologetics. Knowing the truth is essential for apologetics, but there are other volumes in print designed to teach that skill. Yet, Christian apologetics requires a degree of theological knowledge before any serious effort can be made in response to attacks on the faith.

Biblical Beliefs, then, is intended to be a theology book. One could describe it as a book about basic Christian doctrine. It surveys basic biblical beliefs over the course of twelve chapters. Theology, though a broad term, speaks to our knowledge of and response to God's truth. It describes both the content of Scripture as well as our conclusions based upon Scripture. This book is written with the conviction that doctrine matters for all of life.

The word "doctrine" simply means "teaching." It refers specifically to the teachings of Jesus Christ. These are the very words the apostles were committed to transmitting to the next generation for the success of the Gospel. While doctrine includes both beliefs and practices, it is specifically used in the New Testament to describe the truths surrounding the life, death, resurrection, and return of Jesus and their application to life. Jesus Himself prayed near the end of His earthly ministry that His followers would be "sanctified in truth" (John 17:19). While the topic of sanctification will be explained later in this volume, Jesus' words mean that true Christian growth is built only upon the foundation of truth.

This book is designed to give Christians an overview of some of the foundational doctrines upon which the Christian faith has rested historically. Because basic Christian doctrine is aimed toward equipping Christians for every good work (2 Timothy 3:17), it combines truth in the sense of both right thinking (orthodoxy) and right practice (orthopraxy). Christians who are already involved to some degree in a local church engage in Christian practices all the time. They are also urged in sermons, lessons, and devotions to live their faith outside the four walls of the local church. Unfortunately, they don't often possess the doctrinal content that energizes, sustains, shapes, and grounds those activities. Thus, though this volume will make reference to Christian practices, the focus will be on orthodoxy—or the basic Christian teaching that informs those practices.

Accordingly, this book will interact with key scriptural texts at various points. In such instances, readers are encouraged to pursue these passages further. At the conclusion of each chapter, readers will also find two features that may be helpful. First, they will find the endnote citations where particular authors and texts have been used to explain a particular point in the chapter. Second, a few books will be listed that will be helpful for eager readers desiring to learn more. Because some books are more challenging than others, letters will be used to indicate whether a book is best-suited for Beginners (B), Intermediate readers (I), or Advanced students (A).

The study of Christianity is as noble a pursuit as any other. Theology was once known as the queen of the sciences in the European academy. Although it has fallen from favor in many settings, it is still an essential pursuit for those serious about the faith. My goal is for *Biblical Beliefs* to provide believers with the tools for this noble pursuit.

---

[1] Rodney Stark, *The Rise of Christianity: How the Obscure, Marginal Jesus Movement Became the Dominant Religious Force in the Western World in a Few Centuries* (Princeton, NJ: Princeton University Press, 1996).

[2] Robert Louis Wilken, *The Christians as the Romans Saw Them* (New Haven, CT: Yale University Press, 2003).

1

The Authority of Scripture

Arguably the most stunning claim to the ears of modern people is that the Christian God is a talking God. Believing that He exists, is glorious, perfect, powerful, and superior in every way is startling enough. But to claim that this God communicates with human beings is to make a more controversial claim about God, human beings, and the nature of knowledge itself.

Most Christians in the Western world are encountering a growing cynicism about the possibility of finding "the truth." For some, scientific means are seen as the only reliable avenue for finding truth and knowledge. Yet others recognize science's failures to solve the most basic human problems, such as the common cold. They, in turn, rely on their own experiences and intuitions to gain understanding. However, historic Christianity teaches that the source of all truth, knowledge, and wisdom is God Himself. The fact that He has revealed Himself to human beings may be controversial to some, but to Christians it is humbling and challenging.

The belief that God has spoken is known as revelation. Typically we associate this term with the book of the Bible known as Revelation. But revelation is a more specific and important category. It exists in two forms: General and Special. Both are important to our faith.

General Revelation

General revelation is also sometimes known as natural revelation. Creation itself is a means by which God's power and character is displayed—even if to us it is sometimes veiled. One might say that the fingerprints of the architect are all over the blueprints and the finished product as well. As the book of Psalms notes, "The heavens declare the glory of God" (Psalm 19:1). However, the problem is that apart from a clearer word people don't always marvel at creation and think, "What a mighty God!" In truth, those who are already Christians are spiritually able to come to this conclusion. While many early scientists who studied creation did so with the understanding that the object of their study was God's good design, many who have pursued scientific knowledge in the last few hundred years began with different assumptions. Consequently, they have also come to different conclusions.

There is also another general or natural means by which Christians believe God reveals something of His character. Christians believe in an immaterial part of humans called the conscience. This is what the Apostle Paul is referring to in Romans 2 when he says, "For when Gentiles, who do not have the law, by nature do what the law requires, they are a law to themselves, even though they do not have the law. They show that the work of the law is written on their hearts, while their conscience also bears witness..." (Romans 2:14-15a).

Paul is reminding us that even people who may not have a written word from God about right and wrong are lawbreakers. Their conscience convicting them in some way is evidence of their inner knowledge about right and wrong. So, then, a conscience convicting humans of immorality, as well as creation's demon-stration of divine glory and power, are both general—or natural—means of revelation.

Unfortunately, human beings suppress this knowledge of God. Romans 1-2 —the same chapters that speak of general revelation—also testify to its insuf-ficiency. In other words, we need a clearer, more particular word to reveal the truth about God and ourselves. As we will see later, our consciences are imperfect guides to the knowledge of God because of the hardening influence of sin. While general revelation is an important doctrine of the Christian faith, it is ultimately insufficient for our needs. We need a clear and present word to point us to God. This is the role of special revelation.

Special Revelation

The fullest expression of God arrived in a small town around two thousand years ago. His name is Jesus. As Colossians 2:9 teaches, in Christ all the fullness of God dwells bodily. It is in this man—this "God-man"—that God most clearly showed the world who He is. Clearer than any beautiful sunset or glorious con-stellation, Jesus reveals the glory and power of God. Yet what value does this have for people who were not companions of Jesus? What is the significance of this for people who now live thousands of years later and never had the privilege of a single encounter with this Jesus? This is why God communicated His words to prophets and apostles, and then led them to produce a faithful record of His words and deeds in history. This is what we know as Scripture.

The Bible, or more simply "the Book," is a collection of documents known by Christians as Holy Scripture. There are two characteristics of Scripture that readers will encounter. First, it is divided into two "Testaments"—old and new. Another word for testament would be "covenant." It refers to the way God made agreements or promises to His people. Second, and perhaps more obvious, the Bible consists of 66 individual books. Some are historical books describing events that occurred in the lives of God's people. Others are epistles, letters written from one Christian to another believer or group of believers. Some are poetic, which describe spiritual truths using specialized language and imagery. Perhaps the most challenging is prophetic literature, which uses an array of images to communicate truth about promises, judgments, and events. While there are other genres, perhaps the most important points to remember about these various types of Scripture are: (1) sometimes various elements of each will appear together in the same book, and (2) each type of literature merits a careful approach to interpretation.

The Canon

The composition of Scripture occurred over a long period of time. In fact, some biblical scholars and historians suggest it was recorded over a period of two thousand years. When studied closely, it appears that Scripture describes well over three times that length of time. These books gradually were brought together to comprise what is known as the Christian canon. "Canon" simply means "measuring rod." After all, many religious documents have been written and preserved over the centuries. This leads us to ask, "How do we determine what belongs?"

Christian Scripture is unique in that these books: (1) were written by apostles or prophets, (2) have inner consistency with one another, and (3) are the particular ones recognized by the earliest Christian communities who were personally acquainted with the message of Jesus and the apostles. Each of these important characteristics of the Bible will be considered here.

Authorship

The Bible itself testifies to two important truths about its authorship: First, that this is God's Word. So in some sense, He is its author. Second, human authors also wrote the Bible. At first glance, these claims seem to be riddled with contradiction. How could a single book be dually authored? Wouldn't one supersede the other at some point? Some historical, literary, and biblical information help us understand these two truths.

Some Christians are surprised to learn that our English Bible is a fairly new development. Originally, the Old Testament was largely written in Hebrew, with some small portions written in a similar language known as Aramaic. The New Testament was written in the common Greek of the Roman Empire. Over time, Christian leaders and teachers felt an abiding spiritual obligation to translate these documents into the common language of the people. Eventually by the 1500s, this led to the first English translation of the Bible. More translations would emerge based on various convictions about manuscripts, translation philosophy, and cultural issues. Nevertheless, most Bibles that we have today are translations directly from the original languages.

This is important because, while we note peculiarities like writing style and diversity in vocabulary when reading documents in English, it is especially evident in the original languages as well. This shows that various authors clearly contributed to the Bible. Many of the individual books bear the name of their author. Others have a very early tradition of authorship among those in the early church who received these books first. On the basis, then, of historical observations and literary features, the Bible has multiple authors. Yet even Scripture itself makes this assertion.

Second Peter 1:21 states: "For no prophecy was ever produced by the will of man, but men spoke from God as they were carried along by the Holy Spirit." In this single verse, we learn how both God and human agents were involved in the authorship of Scripture. Holy men (prophets and apostles) were led by the Holy Spirit to write particular things. God, then, is the initiator and author of the Bible. It was His will that led to its recording. Yet we also see the human features of the Scriptures indicating that it was not necessarily mechanically dictated. We will return to this question about the Bible's authorship when we consider the doctrine of inspiration.

A Faithful Message

One of the unique features of Scripture is that despite its diversity in style, authorship, and subject, it possesses a certain unity in its message. While there are no doubt seams in the story, the message itself carries with it incredible consistency. Two examples of this unified testimony will aid in demonstrating this harmony.

First, the Old Testament and New Testament both contain historically verifiable information. Some quickly dismiss the Bible as a full of myths and strange imagery. While on the surface this may seem to be the case for modern readers, even the unusual aspects of Scripture are couched within a larger story of events, places, and peoples. While archaeology, for instance, is not necessarily the exact science it often claims to be, it does frequently confirm the reality of biblical places recorded.[1] The Bible itself is presented as a matter of historical fact. This does not mean everything is verifiable using the standards of historical study. It does mean, however, that Christianity and real historical circumstances are not at odds. It is a mistake to think that because the Bible is a religious, or spiritual, book that it is also not historical in nature.

To clarify the point, an early Christian creed (statement of belief) is helpful. One line of the Apostles' Creed states that Jesus "suffered under Pontius Pilate." This is no small detail. Amid all of the theological content of that creed, the authors included something that was not only contained within Scripture, it also is a matter of historical fact. We can go to secular sources and find out about many of the people and places in Scripture, even if we cannot learn Christian doctrine there.

Another example of the historical nature of Scripture is to consider the writers of the four Gospels. Luke begins his Gospel by saying,

> Inasmuch as many have undertaken to compile a narrative of the things that have been accomplished among us, just as those who from the beginning were eyewitnesses and ministers of the word have delivered them to us, it seemed good to me also, having followed all things closely for some time past, to write an orderly account for you...that you may have certainty concerning the things you have been taught.

(Luke 1:1-4)

Luke is showing that his writing bears the features of an eyewitness account in more than one sense. John similarly writes,

> Now Jesus did many other signs in the presence of the disciples, which are not written in this book; but these are written so that you may believe that Jesus is the Christ, the Son of God, and that by believing you may have life in his name.

(John 20:30-31)

Both of these authors present their writings as historical accounts designed to first inform, and second, to convince readers of certain truths. In the words of Francis Schaeffer, "we are not asked to believe [anything] until we have faced the question as to whether this is true on the basis of space-time evidence."[2]

Another example of the Bible's unity relates to the actual message of Scripture. Despite the numerous differences between the Old and New Testaments, they both operate within the same storyline. This story is the creation of the world, the fall of man, God's redemption plan or covenant with humanity, and the total reconciliation of all things when Christ returns. All of the biblical material—whether it be prophecy, proverb, or letter—contributes to this storyline. Ultimately, the person and work of Jesus Christ are what draw together all the loose threads.

Over the years, many authors have offered ways of seeing the big picture of Scripture. Following is one example that treats it as a play with multiple acts:

Act 1—God Establishes His Kingdom: Creation

Act 2—Rebellion in the Kingdom: Fall

Act 3—The King Chooses Israel: Redemption Initiated

Interlude—A Kingdom Story Waiting for an Ending:
The Intertestamental Period

Act 4—The Coming of the King: Redemption Accomplished

Act 5—Spreading the News of the King: The Mission of the Church

Act 6—The Return of the King: Redemption Completed[3]

The books of Scripture constitute this message. Other religious literature may be enjoyable to read, or may even contain some truthful statements. But the Word of God has been given, recorded, and preserved in the form of the Christian Bible. It tells the story of Christ, His creation, and His inaugurated kingdom. As the earliest Christian communities attested, the biblical documents were faithful to the original message.

Tried and True

One aspect of the Bible that troubles some people is that much of it was written after the events in question. In some cases, the events were recorded decades later. Take, for instance, the four Gospels. Mark is often thought to be the earliest among them. Yet even by the most conservative estimates, it was written no earlier the A.D. 60s![4] How can this be a reliable word? How can we know we have the "real Word of God"?

A third feature of Scripture that attests to its authenticity is the manner of its early reception and transmission. We must remember that in ancient times, many cultures were much more oral in their approach to language and communication. This means that they were not in the habit, as we are, of writing everything down on self-adhesive notes and in notebooks. This isn't to say that historical records were not kept. We even find that in the Old Testament God had Moses record the words He had given him to give to the people (Exodus 34:1). But in many other times and places, people were more accustomed to memorizing information and then verbally communicating it to one another. Such cultural and social activity is known as the "oral tradition." To the surprise of many, modern studies into this ancient practice have shown it to have a remarkable degree of accuracy, even by today's standards.

As we will see in a moment, the role of God's Spirit in preserving and transmitting His Word cannot be overlooked. However, the way early Christian communities received and transmitted Scripture is incredibly important. First, they would have been acquainted personally with the teachings of Jesus. If they hadn't lived in His region and heard Him personally, they would have received the message of Christianity from Jesus' disciples who heard the message firsthand. Eyewitness testimony proves to be an important part of the apostles' ministry. Paul, in 1 Corinthians 15, emphasizes the number of eyewitnesses to the risen Christ so that any who doubted His resurrection could go to a personal source for verification.

Second, the early Christian authors constantly refer to "the deposit" of the faith (e.g., 1 Timothy 6:20; 2 Timothy 1:14). This is significant because it shows there was a very clear idea of the message of Christianity. This would have enabled early churches to discern between truth and error because they had an original word from Jesus' ministry to compare with any other message. This is why some documents written in the first and second centuries were accepted as Christian Scripture and others were not.

A final reason why the early Christian communities' interaction with the Bible is important is because they helped to preserve it and transmit it to the next generation. History shows more than one civil or political figure tried to eliminate God's people or copies of the Scripture. However, the original autographs, though we do not have them today, were copied time and time again. Although we often associate monasteries as places simply for prayer and refuge from worldly pleasures, these sites were largely responsible for the diligent and faithful production of copies of the Scripture throughout the centuries. We still have thousands of manuscripts (or copies) that date back to the first few centuries of the church. Although there are small differences among some of them, this mostly reflects insignificant variants. Thankfully, many newer Bibles today include footnotes to inform the reader of these.

What about the Truth?

These facts only provide a general sketch of the background of Scripture. However, when we encounter an ancient document that modern people find either reliable or divisive, the next reasonable question to ask is, "Is it true?" There are three features of Scripture that deal more consistently with the question of its truthfulness. It is to these three that we now turn.

The Truthfulness of Scripture

Inspiration

"Inspiration" is a word often related to a beautiful piece of music or an uplifting speech. There is even a section in many bookstores known as "Inspirational Literature." The *Oxford English Dictionary* states that "inspire" comes from a Latin word that means "to breathe or blow into." The word "inspiration" only appears once in the entire Bible—in 2 Timothy 3:16: "All scripture is given by inspiration of God" (KJV). So the word has been with us for some time. Yet newer translations of the Bible substitute this word with the phrase "God-breathed." The translators are reflecting the literal way the original language reads. Scripture, in other words, has its source in God Himself.

Second Timothy 3 is one of the most important biblical passages that explains the need for Scripture, its aim or purpose, and its content. Whereas 2 Peter 1:21 above includes the human and divine roles in the composition of Scripture, 2 Timothy 3:16 especially points to the divine authorship of the Bible. Scripture has its origin in the mind of God. This is significant because it then raises the question about the character of Scripture. Is this a reliable word, or one riddled with errors? Interpreting the Bible properly is an important way of answering these questions correctly. However, knowing that God is the divine source of "all scripture" (literally, "all the writings") suggests that the character of Scripture rests on the character of God.

Imagine for a moment that two people you know are going to a basketball game that you are unable to attend. Because your favorite team is playing, you have a vested interest in knowing the outcome of the game. Following the game, you have an opportunity to interview both people to find out details from the game. One of the spectators shares his account of what happened. He happens to also be someone you know well—someone who, in the past, has been reliable in your relationship. From afar, you have watched him deal with others in a fair, honest, and truthful way. The second person then shares her version of the game. Her version, while similar in some respect, differs significantly from the previous one. This person's details about the game itself seem to contradict the previous account—even the final score is off by a few points. Perhaps as significant, the second person has been connected with other incidents where lies have been told and persons have been misled. In other words, this person has a reputation for being deceitful. Once we consider the character of these people, it better enables us to determine which account is reliable. The contradictions in stories tell us that someone—or perhaps both—is not being truthful. However, the faithful, honest character of the first person is what allows you to accept his version with reasonable grounds.

The practical application of the illustration is this: a Christian commitment to the inspiration of Scripture means believing Scripture originates with God. For Him to be the author of Scripture means that it must also bear His character. So unless a Christian believes that "deceitful" or "unreliable" are appropriate words to ascribe to the Lord, then believing in Scripture's truthfulness in all it describes, asserts, commands, or denies is a reasonable conviction.

A final important element of biblical inspiration is to recognize that it is "plenary verbal" inspiration. This simply means it is complete and refers to the actual words themselves, not simply thoughts or sentiments. This may seem rather obvious given the previous explanation, yet it is important because it not only represents the explanation of Scripture itself, it also helps to distinguish the historic Christian understanding of inspiration from other forms that later emerged. For instance, some have taught that the Bible's inspiration was simply based on the effect it had on people, not unlike a Shakespearean sonnet or acclaimed opera. Others have argued for a strict mechanical version of inspiration that reduces the biblical writers to robots with no authentic stylistic contribution. Perhaps worst of all, some have argued that the Bible is only partly inspired. However, one can see that this latter version quickly leads to a very arbitrary, weak Bible. After all, who is in the position to know *which parts* are inspired and which are not?

Our discussion of inspiration leads us to consider a closely related feature of Scripture that has provoked furious debate, especially in the second half of the 20th century: Inerrancy.

Inerrancy

Whereas inspiration speaks primarily to the source or origin of Scripture, inerrancy is a term that describes the actual product or content of the Bible. Though complex, a short definition of scriptural inerrancy would be, "the Bible is truthful in its entirety." Yet this claim provokes many objections. For some, it is the very notion of "truthful" that raises issues. For others, any type of human authorship of Scripture seems to rule out the possibility of inerrancy. Space does not permit us to explore all of the objections to inerrancy, but let's consider some responses to these two key objections.

This is where interpretation is crucial regarding the question of truth. We must understand what a text says and what it means before we can assess if it is true. For example, Jesus says in Matthew 12:34, "You brood of vipers!" Is Jesus really speaking to snakes? No. Therefore, do we conclude the Bible is errant? Of course not. We read the passage and learn He is speaking to Pharisees who are filled with hatred, jealousy, and every other form of bad fruit inconsistent with the heart of God's true people. We understand that "vipers" is figurative language, not meant to be taken literally. This example is illustrative of a larger point: Something can be true in more than one sense. The Bible utilizes an array of language that touches all aspects of the divine-human experience. Therefore, we must understand that doctrines like inerrancy are situated alongside other important Christian practices, such as careful Bible study, sound interpretation, and knowledge of background issues. More will be said on this later.

The other common objection to inerrancy pertains to the human role in authorship. It seems inconceivable that a book authored by a human being would be free from error. However, we must remember 2 Peter 1:21, which reminds us that these authors were "carried along by the Holy Spirit." God's Spirit is related to the direct authoring of Scripture in a number of other passages as well. Examples from both Testaments abound.

Often in the prophetic literature, for instance, God communicates His truth to human authors directly through vision or oracle (e.g., Ezekiel 1:1; Isaiah 6:8). Also, in John 14–17, we read of Jesus' final words of instruction, encouragement, and warning to His disciples before dying. His word of promise includes what we read in John 14:25-26: "These things I have spoken to you while I am still with you. But the Helper, the Holy Spirit, whom the Father will send in my name, he will teach you all things and bring to your remembrance all that I have said to you." These are just a few of the many passages that assure any modern reader that God provides the means for His truth to pass reliably from one generation to the next.

Many Christians do indeed stumble, however, when their experience of Scripture seems to contradict what they read in books such as this. They come across four Gospels and wonder why the early apostles couldn't seem to get their stories straight about Jesus. Yet, let's consider another illustration to help understand this important point.

Imagine a horrific automobile accident has happened at a busy intersection in a major city. Because you were not physically present to witness it, you tune-in to the evening news to learn more. If you watch the accounts from several news networks, you will notice that no two are exactly the same. They will all contain many of the same basic details, of course, such as the parties involved, the location, and perhaps even the cause of the accident. But some of these reports will leave out parts that others include. They will differ in length, emphasis, and even tone. Yet it is entirely possible that the bare facts reported are in no way lies. They are simply told through the lens of different reporters and different eyewitnesses who saw or experienced the accident from different vantage points.

While this is an imperfect illustration because it doesn't involve divine inspiration, it does help us understand the nature of Scripture's faithfulness. There are indeed other reasonable questions that can be asked about Scripture, many of which have already been taken up by Christian teachers throughout the centuries. It is important, though, for us to see that the Bible's divine inspiration ensures its inerrancy. Consequently, its inerrancy ensures its infallibility.

Infallibility

Some Christians who reject the inerrancy of Scripture have often gravitated more toward the adjective "infallible." They think that this word better describes the content of Scripture. Calling it "infallible" means we acknowledge that Scripture will not fail to accomplish its intended purpose. For such individuals, this often becomes a subtle way of implying that Scripture is only good for "religious and spiritual purposes." However, it is unreliable on matters relating to geography, history, culture, and related matters.

This approach is problematic on several grounds. First, it doesn't take seriously the very words of Paul. He says in 2 Timothy that "all Scripture," not "some Scripture" is inspired of God. Second, this view often subjects Scripture to a very narrow standard for what constitutes accuracy or truthfulness. For instance, this is seen in the numbers often given. Most often the Bible gives round numbers to describe groups of people, like 5,000 or 300. Naturally, in the same way we give a ballpark figure when dealing with larger numbers, the biblical authors did the same.

Some would suggest that examples like imprecise numbers make the Bible errant. Yet most reasonable persons understand that the everyday language employed by the biblical authors squares with the normal experience of human beings in all times. Using modern standards to judge ancient documents that are shaped by cultural features is a poor way to judge truthfulness. Yet evangelicals need not fear the word "infallible." It is absolutely true that because the Bible is from God (inspiration), it is truthful in every sense (inerrancy). And because it is truthful, it will never mislead or fail to accomplish its purpose (infallibility).

Understanding and Trusting Scripture

Before some explanation is given on the important task of biblical interpretation, a word of encouragement is due to those who find themselves overwhelmed by the challenges of understanding and trusting Scripture. Most Christians do not become believers after a prolonged study of the critical questions about the Bible. Typically they were raised in a Christian home, reared in church, and eventually became convinced that they were sinners in need of rescue. It is only later that their Christian journey led them to this present set of issues.

For those wanting a place to provide greater assurance about the authority and trustworthiness of the Scriptures, they can look to the very words of their Savior, Jesus Christ. Many of the objections raised against a historic, orthodox understanding of the Bible could be answered if we point to the chief character in Scripture. The life and ministry of Christ offers a useful guide for how His people should handle Scripture.

First, Jesus seems to establish a canon. In His ministry, He frequently quoted from the Old Testament. He most often utilized Isaiah, Psalms, and portions of the law. This is seen especially in His Sermon on the Mount (Matthew 5–7). He even offers what we might call "hints for interpretation" because of how He uses and explains other passages. Second, Jesus confirms this by His citation of specific figures and events from the Old Testament. In particular, He refers to the lives and words of Noah, Abraham, Moses, David, and many others. He also establishes Abel through Zechariah as a sort of prophetic line (Matthew 23:35). Jesus, then, is no stranger to the Scriptures. In the same way that John 1:1-4 teaches us that He was "the Word," He also affirms our confidence in the written Word.

Interpretation

There are many useful resources available in the area known as "hermeneutics," or simply, biblical interpretation. Hermeneutics is related to the name of the Greek god Hermes who delivered and interpreted messages. In the course of our communication with other people, we quickly realize that what they say, what they mean, and the aim of their words are all distinct parts of communication. The example from Jesus' encounter with the Pharisees above illustrates this point. Because biblical interpretation is such a large topic with many individual issues, three basic principles for interpretation will be offered here. Further reading on this topic can be found at the end of the chapter.

First, we must answer the question, *"Where* is this particular verse or passage?" The meaning of words arises from within a context. In most cases, when reading a passage, we need to determine *who* is writing the verse. *To whom* are they writing? *What* are the circumstances under which they are writing? Only when these basic questions are answered can we understand the original purpose of a given statement.

Second, we must answer the question, "What does this text *say*?" This seems like an obvious point, but it is often overlooked. Knowing what it says usually involves some digging beneath the surface. It is closely related to the third question, "What does this verse or passage *mean*?" When Paul says, "Greet one another with a holy kiss"(e.g. Romans 16:16), we have to determine what a holy kiss is. Sometimes we must go deeper to determine if "kiss" is the same as how we understand "kiss" in 21st-century America. Because the Bible was originally written in languages other than English, using different tools such as lexicons and dictionaries is helpful. Also, because of the cultural differences between the biblical world and the modern world, resources such as Bible commentaries are often very important. Most church libraries have these, or they can also be easily purchased at a Christian bookstore. While these three questions are only initial steps, they are important ones to interpret Scripture.

Whether we are preparing a lesson to teach or simply trying to find an answer to a co-worker's challenging question, it is a spiritual obligation to study the Word. Therefore, we should avail ourselves of every means to understand the Scriptures. Many Christians during the Protestant Reformation emphasized the "perspicuity of Scripture." This means that Scripture is designed so it would be clear enough to be studied and obeyed. This does not mean there aren't challenging passages. It does mean that God was speaking to Israel and He speaks to us when He says, "This commandment...is not too hard for you, neither is it far off" (Deuteronomy 30:11).

Authority

What drives the decisions you make? Human beings make thousands of decisions every day. Obviously, most of them aren't life-altering in any way. Yet they range from what color shirt or blouse we will wear, to the college or spouse we choose. Whatever drives these decisions is a source of authority. For Christians, this authority is the Bible.

Another way of understanding the authority that Scripture should have in both the church and the Christian life is by thinking of Scripture as sufficient. In defending this, it does not mean that Scripture is a comprehensive guide to every fact about the universe. The Bible, though without error, was not primarily intended to be a college admissions guide or a map for traveling through the Middle East. Scripture as God's Word is intended to reveal the truth about God's character, will, and ways. It is designed to show people the way to spiritual transformation through Christ.

However, the temptation will always exist for Christians to abandon or diminish Scripture's ability to provide sure counsel for navigating all areas of life and ministry. As politicians use polling data to chart their likeability and policy decisions, pastors may rely on extra-biblical information to lead their congregations. Parents will be inclined to trust popular psychologists from television in rearing their children. Those in dire financial straits may look to security blankets like credit cards. Scripture speaks to all of these matters—church leadership, family life, and financial stewardship. While all truth is God's truth wherever it may be found, Scripture is the surest and most sufficient guide Christians can—and should—look to for wisdom that honors God when it is obeyed.

Summary

God has revealed His character and glory in creation. When we look at it carefully, it causes believers to marvel, provoking worship and obedience since we know the architect behind the design and beauty we see. The Lord, knowing the depth of our sin and the needs of His people, provided them with an even surer word—the Scriptures and His Son. As Hebrews 1:1-2a helpfully summarizes, "Long ago, at many times and in many ways, God spoke to our fathers by the prophets, but in these last days he has spoken to us by his Son." The words of Christ have been faithfully recorded by His apostles and are addressed to the human heart by the Holy Spirit Himself.

Christians living in the 21st century share something crucially in common with God's people of old. They both faced the same fundamental temptation: to reject the Word of God. As we will see in chapter three, the first humans God created were tempted by a being who effectively convinced them that their Creator had deceived them with His instructions. Their doubt led to disobedience. In the same way, Christians today will continue to encounter questions, challenges, and even animosity as they rely on the Scriptures. The crucial challenge will be for them to better understand the Bible so they can answer honest questions and defend it against misconstrued objections. Most importantly, however, their very lives will communicate to those around them whether or not God's Word is truly authoritative and life-changing. The Word, we might say, shows God's will and ways. When obeyed, it leads to witness and worship.

For Further Reading:

Frame, John. *The Doctrine of the Word of God*. Phillipsburg, NJ: P&R Publishing, 2010. **(B)**

Goldsworthy, Graeme. *According to Plan: The Unfolding Revelation of God in the Bible*. Downers Grove, IL: IVP Academic, 1991. **(B)**

Plummer, Robert. *40 Questions on Interpreting the Bible*. Grand Rapids, MI: Kregel Academic, 2010. **(B)**

Ward, Timothy. *Words of Life: Scripture as the Living and Active Word of God*. Downers Grove, IL: IVP Academic, 2009. **(I)**

Warfield, B. B. *The Inspiration and Authority of the Bible*. Phillipsburg, NJ: P & R Publishing, 1980. **(I)**

Wenham, John. *Christ and the Bible*. Eugene, OR: Wipf & Stock Publishers, 2009. **(I)**

---

[1] Matthew J. McAffee, "Can Archaeology Deliver?" *Helwys Society Forum,* March 7, 2011, accessed July 25, 2012, http://www.helwyssocietyforum.com/?p=100.

[2] Francis A. Schaeffer, *The God Who Is There: Speaking Historic Christianity into the Twentieth Century* (Downers Grove, IL: InterVarsity Press, 1968), 141.

[3] Craig G. Bartholomew and Michael W. Goheen, *The Drama of Scripture: Finding Our Place in the Biblical Story* (Grand Rapids, MI: Baker Academic, 2004), 7.

[4] Craig L. Blomberg, *Jesus and the Gospels: An Introduction and Survey* (Nashville, TN: Broadman & Holman, 1997), 123.

2

The Godhead

A.W. Tozer begins his classic book, *The Knowledge of the Holy*, with these words: "What comes into our minds when we think about God is the most important thing about us." [1] This is certainly true for Christians. As we will see throughout this book, our foundational convictions about God will inform and shape how we understand and approach other doctrines. However, our views of God also have the potential to undermine faithful Christian living when Scripture doesn't inform them. Therefore, the doctrine of God is at the center of Christian theology.

Considering God's existence and nature is also relevant because very few people are apathetic about the topic. Though some remain agnostic or unsure of God's existence, most Americans profess belief in some God. Unfortunately, this "God" isn't always the Christian God. For believers, perhaps the most important reason why our theology, or words about God, must be meaningful and coherent is because the main actor in the biblical drama is God Almighty. He is the object of our worship, and so it is essential to understand who He is.

The Great Three-in-One

Complex machines are impossible to understand apart from how they actually work. In the case of people, we best understand them by not merely gazing at them from afar or from reading personal profiles. We look at *what they do*. God is similar in this respect. In order to grasp His person, looking at His marvelous works is of great importance. People often point to the Psalms, Israel's hymnal, for words that exalt the Lord God. However, one quickly notices as they peruse this book that the psalmists almost always name specific acts that ground their praise. In uncovering the biblical portrait of God, we find that the brushstrokes are His mighty deeds. Understanding this relationship between God's person and His deeds is helpful for setting the stage for our study of Him, and particularly His triune character.

The most complex and important truth about the Christian God is that He is triune. The "Trinity" is a reference to the fact that God exists eternally in three persons: God the Father, God the Son, and God the Holy Spirit. Though they are one in their essence, they are three in person. As challenging as this is to grasp, the most helpful way Christians can begin to make sense of it is by seeing what each member of the Trinity does. This is why chapters four and five will be devoted specifically to the person and work of Christ and the Spirit. Our attention here will be more generally on the attributes of God. But we must gain an initial understanding of the Trinitarian God that Christians believe in.

It is difficult to understand America's economy apart from evaluating interest rates, employment numbers, and other financial factors. Similarly, it is also impossible to reflect upon the Trinitarian God apart from understanding the "economy of salvation" (see chapter six). This language refers to the various acts of the Godhead to make salvation possible. As we consider these events, it better enables us to understand both the "oneness of God" and the "three-ness of God." The good news for Christians baffled by the Trinity is that God is who He is apart from what we know. As Fred Sanders notes, "Reality comes first, and understanding follows it."[2] This means that Christians, regardless of where they are in their journey, already have some unspoken understanding of the members of the Godhead. Again, Sanders helpfully states, "We need to see and feel that we are surrounded by the Trinity, compassed about on all sides by the presence and the work of the Father, the Son, and the Holy Spirit."[3]

Christian teachers have made numerous efforts throughout the centuries to better help lay Christians to understand the biblical accounts of the Trinity—especially since the Bible never uses this precise term. There are at least three key dimensions of the Trinity that believers should start with: (1) they share the same character and attributes; (2) they work in concert with one another; (3) they perform different functions. Let's briefly consider how these three relate.

There is a reason why they bear the names that they do. God reveals Himself using this familial language because it in some way designates a relationship among the Godhead. Yet it is not a 1:1 ratio with human relationships. Just because there is a Son doesn't mean He is necessarily younger than the Father, nor does it mean the Spirit is "out of the loop" since He does not bear a personal name. While the Father biblically is the member from whom the Son is begotten and from whom the Spirit proceeds, He is not older or more "God-like" in His being. They are equal in power, glory, and honor. They stand eternally in fellowship with one another, never dissenting in opinion or will. Yet when it comes to salvation, for instance, God the Father gives the Son, who becomes the incarnate Son: Jesus Christ. The Spirit helps the virgin Mary conceive Jesus, and then leads Him, anoints Him, and fills Him for His earthly ministry.

Probably the best biblical passage to see these three in concert is Jesus' baptism:

> In those days Jesus came from Nazareth of Galilee and was baptized by John in the Jordan. And when he came up out of the water, immediately he saw the heavens being torn open and the Spirit descending on him like a dove. And a voice came from heaven, "You are my beloved Son; with you I am well pleased."
>
> (Mark 1:9-11)

Passages such as this make it obvious that all three cooperate in their work, though it is distinct. More of the Godhead's function will be seen in later chapters.

Attributes: God Alone

Typically, when theologians and biblical scholars have written about the nature of God, they have described Him using two sets of characteristics—those that belong to Him alone and those that characterize Him and should, to some extent, characterize His people. Obviously God's triune existence is unique to Him. No other religion understands God as evangelical Christians do. Yet what else has God revealed about Himself in Scripture? Here we will consider a few of the clearest elements of the doctrine of God.

What's in a Name?

Names carry great significance to us. Souvenir shops are filled with trinkets donning the more common names in American culture at the particular moment. Athletes bear their last names on the back of their uniforms. We are annoyed when someone misspells our name. We do this because our names matter to us. They represent us. They are how we introduce ourselves to one another. It is how we are known. In the ancient Hebrew culture, the case was similar. The naming of a child was often tied to some sort of future blessing, prediction, or specific circumstance surrounding the child's birth. Throughout the Bible, names carry significance. Abraham, for example, means "Father of many nations." This is eventually true when we study the course of history. Being in a position to name someone else signals some privileged place of power, knowledge, or authority. We will see this further in chapter three when we see Adam given the task of naming the earthly creatures.

When it comes to God, however, we aren't in any position to know Him, let alone give Him a name apart from His revelation. This is why the Old Testament uses several names to refer to the same God. These notes sound slightly different, yet they all contribute to the melody that says, "Yahweh is Lord." Yahweh is a form of the verb "to be." But God saying to Moses, "I AM WHO I AM" (Exodus 3:14) has puzzled biblical scholars. Most, however, return to some idea of this being a sign of God's self-sufficiency. He cannot be surmised in a conventional Hebrew name. Most English translations refer to this name when they say the "LORD" or "the LORD God." This is no generic deity. He is the God of Israel, but as we see His power displayed, the nations come to see He is the one true and living God. In His encounters throughout the pages of Old Testament—and then particularly in the New—we see many things that describe His greatness. While space is limited here, we will look at some specific attributes of God in the Bible.

Omniscience

Psalm 139 is perhaps the single best passage in Scripture that displays several of God's most awesome features. In particular, the God of heaven is an *all-knowing God*. That is to say, He is omniscient. This speaks to the comprehensive range of His knowledge, whether it concerns persons, places, events, or any other created thing. David says,

> O LORD, you have searched me and known me! You know when I
> sit down and when I rise up; you discern my thoughts from afar.
> You search out my path and my lying down and are acquainted
> with all my ways (vv. 1-3).

David's God knows him intimately—this is personal knowledge that a close friend might possess. But it is much more than this. God knows the number of hairs on our head (Matthew 10:30). He even knows the intentions of our hearts (e.g., 1 Samuel 16:7; 1 Corinthians 4:5). God's knowledge, then, brings awe and fear.

God's knowledge also functions in reference to time. Admittedly, God's relationship to time is a complex subject in Christian theology. However, it is relevant because God is portrayed as One not forcefully bound by created dimensions, such as space and time. That He chooses to operate with us in this way, namely in Jesus Christ and the Holy Spirit, is a gift. But time is pertinent to what God knows because Scripture teaches God's foreknowledge. It is one thing to say that He knows me individually as a creature. It is another stunning claim to assert that He knows the future!

Some Christians have argued that God knows the future because He predetermines it. Others contend that God's foreknowledge is simple—that it has no causal affect on the actual outcome of things. Both perspectives fog the mind as it tries to mull them over. In truth, both are perspectives that have been adopted by conservative Christians. However, both agree that God knows the past, present, and future comprehensively. Christians who are interested in this topic are encouraged to look closely at their church's doctrinal statement, or survey other Christian literature that discusses these topics.[4]

Omnipotence

That God is "all-powerful" seems rather self-evident. After all, most people would not ascribe divinity to a being that was limited. David speaks of God's power to create in Psalm 139:13-14: "For you formed my inward parts; you knitted me together in my mother's womb. I praise you, for I am fearfully and wonderfully made. Wonderful are your works; my soul knows it very well." We will further consider God's power in creation in the next chapter, but here, two observations will suffice.

First, God's power is without limit. There is nothing outside of Himself that restricts what He is able to do. This obviously defies the pride of the human race. The Apostle Paul even says that while creation should be an adequate witness to His great power, humans suppress this truth (Romans 1:20-21). It is for this reason that some unbelieving skeptics have concocted silly scenarios to challenge God's power, such as, "Can God make a rock He cannot lift?" Besides the wrong spirit in which the question is asked, it also overlooks the harmonious nature of God's character. His perfection, for example, wouldn't lead Him to exercise His power in a way that conflicts with either His character or will.

Second, God's power is further evidence that He is a sovereign God. Sovereignty means "the power to rule." A sovereign ruler is able to do as he freely chooses. However, to accomplish this there must be some sort of power accompanying either his character or his rank. God's ability to rule (His sovereignty) derives in part from His omnipotence. Court jesters aren't sovereign because they aren't omnipotent in the kingdom. Military lieutenants, though respected among their fellow soldiers, aren't sovereign because they aren't all-powerful. Only a king can be sovereign. This king is the Lord God.

Omnipresence

We aren't present everywhere, despite what many of our modern technologies cause us to think. We may indeed think that because we can communicate across state and national boundaries in the blink of an eye we are omnipresent. Once again, note David's words from Psalm 139:

> Where shall I go from your Spirit? Or where shall I flee from your presence? If I ascend to heaven, you are there! If I make my bed in Sheol, you are there! If I take the wings of the morning and dwell in the uttermost parts of the sea, even there your hand shall lead me, and your right hand shall hold me (vv. 7-10).

In a prior age, it was perhaps difficult to grasp omnipresence because we only think of presence in terms of physical presence. In other words, presence was reduced to where our bodies could be. But today, many tend to deny this. This is, however, different from God's omnipresence.

The Bible teaches that God not only creates the world, but He upholds it by His very Word (e.g., Hebrews 1:2; Colossians 1:16). Thus, it naturally follows that He oversees the world. He is able to oversee it because He is infinite (see the following). God is not limited in His essence, so He is able to be fully present everywhere. This is not to say God, as some New Age religions teach, spiritually inhabits rocks, trees, and other created things. God is indeed a spirit according to Scripture (John 4:24). However, because He is not bound to a particular space in His essence, He is capable of forming a relationship with His creation and providentially overseeing it.

This brings fear, humility, and comfort to a believer, but anxiety to the one who tries to escape the knowledge of God. We also see in this doctrine how omniscience and omnipotence operate in relation to one another. God's knowledge, power, and presence all work in conjunction to make Him the sovereign ruler that He is.

Immutability

"Theology proper" (the doctrine of God) is partly challenging because in it, we find so much about the Lord that is unlike us. Immutability is as foreign to human beings as anything else. To be immutable is to be unchangeable. Human beings, however, change constantly. We age. We grow. We change opinions and appetites seamlessly from moment to moment. This is why the immutability of God is presented in Scripture as a means to provoke obedience to God's commands, which flow from an unchangeable nature and provide comfort to frail human beings. Consider the following passages:

Numbers 23:19 – "God is not man, that he should lie, or a son of man, that he should change his mind....Or has he spoken, and will he not fulfill it?"

Malachi 3:6 – "For I the LORD do not change; therefore you,
O children of Jacob, are not consumed."

James 1:17 – "Every good gift and every perfect gift is from above,
coming down from the Father of lights with whom there is
no variation or shadow due to change."

In these few verses, God's immutability is connected with His faithfulness, His truthfulness, and His promises. His unchangeable character is as much about

His character as it is about His actions. God, in other words, does not change because His character is one of perfect love, faithfulness, as well as power and wisdom. While He is free to do as He likes, God willingly enters relationships with people that necessarily means He deals with us in ways that may, at least on the surface, result in change. But a change in His response does not reflect a change in His essence or character.

There is a final note about biblical interpretation one should bear in mind, especially in reference to immutability. In Scripture, God is sometimes portrayed as silent, distant, or altogether absent. In other instances, He is said to have "remembered" (cf. Exodus 2:24). Still in others, He is said to have "changed his mind" or "relented" (e.g., Exodus 32:14; Amos 7:3). In these instances, the biblical authors, though inspired by God, use what is called "phenomenal language." They are writing on how things *appear to be*. This is likely intended for us, such that frail human beings reading the Bible today could benefit from the insight of other frail human beings who faithfully recorded their experiences with God. This is a reminder to us of both our weaknesses and God's kindness to us by operating with us in a dynamic, personal experience. In other words, He is a personal God who responds to human action, need, and prayer.

Personal and Infinite

We conclude our discussion of the attributes unique to God with two that are in tension yet affirmed in Scripture: personal and infinite. These reflect two incredible truths. On the one hand, God is not distant and aloof from the affairs of human beings. He is unlike the god of many prominent thinkers of the late 17th and 18th centuries who believed in a god who creates but who doesn't care. This is a personal God who hears prayers, receives worship, and providentially oversees what happens in the universe. It is overwhelming that a great God exists who involves Himself in the messy affairs of human life. This is seen most powerfully in His sending of the Son, Christ Jesus.

On the other hand, God is infinite. This, by definition, means He is unlimited in every sense of the word. He is beyond the complete comprehension of anyone or anything outside of Himself. There is no developing technology that will finally "figure Him out." The human mind reaches a point where it can go no further. Of course, because God is personal, He gives us His very Spirit to help us make sense of His Word. Even still, our capacities fail us. This is where our consideration of God's noncommunicable attributes ends and surveying His communicable attributes begins.

Attributes: God and His Will for Us

There is a second class of characteristics that God perfectly possesses. Yet what makes these unique from the aforementioned attributes is that they are ones God's people are also called to possess. They are sometimes known as "communicable attributes." Some of the more prominent ones in Scripture will be explained.

Holiness

God's most fundamental moral quality is His holiness. Sacrifices were brought into the tabernacle to a special place known as "the Most Holy Place." Entering such a place with caution and specific procedures reflected the utter holiness of Israel's God. He was without taint, impurity, or moral defect. And yet even He called His people to the same pattern of character. He says in Leviticus 11:44, "For I am the LORD your God. Consecrate yourselves therefore, and be holy, for I am holy." He proceeds in verse 45 to say, "For I am the LORD who brought you up out of the land of Egypt to be your God. You shall therefore be holy, for I am holy."

God's holiness forms the basis of His commands and laws to His people. Even for New Testament Christians, the holiness language of the Old Testament is applied. For something or someone to be holy means for it to be "set apart for special use." Other features, such as purity, are associated with it. As we will see in chapter seven, the Christian life is a project in purification that the Spirit brings to bear upon us (e.g., Titus 2:11-14). The apostles pick up the same thread very clearly in their writings (e.g., 1 Peter 1:16). Because Christians belong to the Lord and are His children, their lives should reflect His holy character as well. As children are often identified with their parents by virtue of their facial features, gestures, and habits, our heavenly Father expects the same from us. We are told, in fact, that without it, no one will see the Lord (Hebrews 12:14).

Holiness is a fundamental attribute of God, if not the most foundational. His other attributes, His moral demands, and even His actions toward human beings in the Bible and today flow out of His holy character. This is to say that He is right and just in all He does because He never violates His moral purity. While human standards for morality may be held high in some families, churches, or even secular organizations, they are never more upright than His. More will be said later on how this connects to other doctrines of the faith.

Love

It is no accident that the first song many children learn is "Jesus Loves Me." For many of those same children, John 3:16 is the first Bible verse they memorize. Both of these express the depth and extent of God's love. God is love. It doesn't reduce God to the idea of love, though many in the 1960s came to see spirituality through this lens. What kind of love is this divine love?

God in eternity past was perfectly content. The members of the Trinity dwelled in harmony amongst one another. There was no lack of love among them that led God out of dissatisfaction to create human beings. However, it was indeed an extravagant love that led Him to bestow the gift of life to human beings. In creation alone, we see the love of God shown to creatures that otherwise would not have existed.

In the biblical storyline, we quickly see that God's love does not trump His holiness. In the earliest chapters of Scripture, when mankind begins to go astray and God's holiness is seemingly undermined, this loving God both judges wickedness and yet always spares a remnant. Love is then associated with God's grace (unmerited favor) and mercy (forbearance).

Ultimately the apex of Scripture is the coming of Jesus Christ. Because God Himself stepped into human affairs by the second member of the Trinity coming to die for the sins of many—including ones who would reject Him—this shows that God's love is a self-giving, sacrificial love. The biblical authors link this love with grace in numerous places, so we see how these attributes are closely related. We will consider grace more carefully in chapter six.

Possessing and showing God's love is no easier than that of holiness. However, it is also clearly the mark of the Christian:

> Little children, yet a little while I am with you. You will seek me, and just as I said to the Jews, so now I also say to you, "Where I am going you cannot come." A new commandment I give to you, that you love one another: just as I have loved you, you also are to love one another. By this all people will know that you are my disciples, if you have love for one another.

> (John 13:33-35)

Jesus will, in another place, refer to love for God as the first and greatest commandment and love for neighbor as the second, similar commandment. It is through love that we mirror the character of our Creator.

Justice

Perhaps the most troubling image of God that we see in both the Old and New Testaments is that of Him being a judge. He is called the "righteous judge" (2 Timothy 4:8). Judges are charged with upholding the law. They are charged with dispensing justice. The problem is that human courts will always fail to perfectly administer justice. But there is perhaps a deeper problem than potentially dishonest attorneys, witnesses, and judges. Our own laws, or standards of justice, may be in error.

This is where we discover another close theological relationship among God's attributes. His holy standards are the basis for His justice. This is why God is compelled to both reward the righteous and punish the wicked. Yet His law is the basis for those judgments. It is only in Christ that anyone ever can meet the righteous requirements of His law (see chapter four).

This raises a more important consideration that readers must keep in mind. The mind of God is not divided into compartments, as it were. For instance, love, holiness, and justice are all attributes of His that work in perfect concert with one another. They function in such a way that they never cause His actions to be inconsistent. An illustration will better help to make this point.

We often say of a good person who has perhaps done something questionable, "They were acting out of character." This expression is our way of accounting for the moral gap between who we know or believe someone to be and his or her actions. The only problem with this expression is that it can only be applied to weak, frail human beings. God never acts "out of character." His deeds are always consistent with His character. His will and even His promises never arise out of a passing bad temper or oversight on His part. They are holy and just. This is why Christians will need a biblical understanding of God's justice if they are to later make sense of doctrines like justification, hell, and others.

God's people are called to be just in their dealings with others (e.g., Micah 6:8; 1 Corinthians 5:12). This is especially true among members of the church. We must be a community committed to holiness and standing for justice if we are to properly heed Christ's warning, which is to be careful in our judgments, lest we find ourselves judged in the same manner (i.e., Matthew 7:1-2). More will be said on this subject when we arrive at chapters eight and nine.

Other Moral Attributes

There are other characteristics about God worth considering. Scripture certainly teaches of other moral attributes beyond those mentioned here. But many of them are best seen by peering into the life of Christ and the work of the Spirit. After all, if Jesus is the image of the invisible God, then this means that in Him, we glimpse the very character of God. In the same way, if the Spirit is God who is with us in living the Christian life, then we should expect that He would help us demonstrate characteristics like holiness, love, mercy, patience, and many other "fruits of the Spirit." It is true that God is patient, kind, merciful, and complete in every other moral good one can possess. But it is encouraging to know that in Christ, through the Spirit, He is able and willing to help us strive for these as well.

Conclusion

"Awesome" is a word often tossed about in our contemporary time. Unfortunately, its present-day usage often diminishes its most appropriate reference—the Lord God. Leroy Forlines captures this concern best:

> It is true that God is "remarkable," "mind-boggling," or "extraordinary." But, as we have seen, these words do not get at the heart of what is meant by either the biblical or the historical use of the word "awesome" as it was used in the English language....Perhaps the best solution for the problem will be for us to make frequent and *proper* [italics mine] use of words like awesome and holy. We need to confront people with that view of God that Moses, Isaiah, and Paul had when they were encountered by God as told in Exodus 3:6; Isaiah 6:5; and Acts 9:3....When the Christian is confronted with the true awesomeness of God, he or she will be ready for true worship and true service.[5]

Forlines is responding to the concern that many times, our language falls short of its intended goal. Ultimately, a word like "awesome" doesn't best describe a T-shirt, a pair of sneakers, or even a sports car. It is most fitting for a God like the one described here.

Of course, our words often fall short. Our language about God is largely analogical—that is, it describes Him using more familiar categories He has given us, such as "Father," "King," and "Master." But our speech about God is always subservient to God's speech about Himself to us through His Spirit and in the Son. Keeping this crucial truth in mind not only helps us to be doctrinally sound, but also spiritually humble.

There is a great deal more that can be said about the Lord God. However, more discussion is not provided for one of two reasons. First, some related issues are reserved for discussion in later chapters. More in reference to the triune God will be said in chapters four and five, while God's freedom will be considered in the next chapter. But second, the danger always exists for human beings to attempt to say more about God than He has said to us concerning Himself. This is likely what Moses meant in Deuteronomy 29:29: "The secret things belong to the LORD our God, but the things that are revealed belong to us and to our children forever, that we may do all the words of this law." Therefore, we carefully attend to the truth God has given us. This is obviously why books such as this are written. However, where we lack understanding, we obey the revealed word and pray for more wisdom to obey this mighty, sovereign God.

For Further Reading:

Packer, J. I. *Knowing God.* Downers Grove, IL: InterVarsity Press, 1973. **(B)**

Tozer, A. W. *The Knowledge of the Holy.* San Francisco: HarperCollins, 1961. **(B)**

Wells, David F. *God in the Wasteland: The Reality of Truth in a World of Fading Dreams.* Grand Rapids, MI: Eerdmans, 1994. **(A)**

---

[1] A. W. Tozer, *The Knowledge of the Holy* (San Francisco: HarperCollins, 1961), 7.

[2] Fred Sanders, *The Deep Things of God: How the Trinity Changes Everything* (Wheaton, IL: Crossway, 2010), 27.

[3] Ibid., 34.

[4] Perhaps the best treatment on two major views that relate to foreknowledge and predestination is Robert E. Picirilli's *Grace, Faith, and Free Will: Contrasting Views of Salvation* (Nashville, TN: Randall House, 2002).

[5] F. Leroy Forlines, *The Quest for Truth: Answering Life's Inescapable Questions* (Nashville, TN: Randall House, 2001), 79.

3

Creation and the Fall

How can the world be filled with such beauty and splendor, and yet also such devastation and distress? On a clear evening, many people walk onto their back porches, gaze into the sky, and are awed by the sight of stars. Yet many others walk onto their back porches and hear the sounds of domestic abuse next door. Many live in squalor, while others are able—by the dignity of an honest day's labor—to bring home a paycheck. How is it that these contrasting pictures are simultaneously observed in our world?

Christianity gives an account of these experiences. It is in the Bible's account of the creation of the world and its fall that we are able to make sense of our origin and our predicament. Understanding the origin of the universe is a worthwhile subject because it helps us glimpse the way God intended things to be. In His creation, His glory and goodness are seen and experienced. But living in a creation ravaged by the fallout of human disobedience reminds us who we are as human beings. It reminds us of our deepest brokenness that only God is capable of mending. That redemption will be considered further in chapter four. Yet for now, we will consider what Graham Cole calls "the glory and garbage of the universe."[1]

Creation: God's Good Gift

While the specifics of the creation event are debated in some Christian circles, there are three truths that bind together historic Christianity: (1) creation came out of nothing; (2) creation was spoken into existence; and (3) creation was very good. Each of these, while obvious enough on the basis of Genesis 1–2, merits further explanation and reflection.

Christian thought throughout the centuries has adopted many Latin words and expressions. One of the most familiar is *ex nihilo*, which refers to the fact that God created everything out of nothing. Time, space, matter, and energy, as we know them, seem to emerge out of this creative act. In earlier days of scientific thought, some, such as Albert Einstein, believed that the universe was static and eternal. However, his own theory of general relativity only confirmed what the Bible had long taught—that there was "a definite beginning to all time, all matter, and all space."[2]

As a feature of creation, *ex nihilo*—God's creative act—was verbal in nature. This coincides with the plenary verbal view of inspiration set forth earlier. God's word is capable of accomplishing what it sets out to accomplish. In this case, it is a creating word. This is later supported by what is seen in other passages. For instance, in the prophets, God is shown to be capable of breathing new life into the spiritually dead (cf. Ezekiel 36). Also, Hebrews 1:1-4 reminds us of Christ the Son's role in a close correlate of creation: providence. It says he "upholds the universe by the word of his power." As we will see in chapter four, "by him all things were created, in heaven and on earth, visible and invisible" (Colossians 1:16a). Because Jesus is called "the Word" in John 1, seeing Him as co-equal with the Father in creation makes perfect sense. In fact, the word "universe" literally means "single, spoken sentence."

The final feature of creation—its intrinsic goodness—is evidenced by the refrain of Genesis 1: "And God saw that it was good." This reflects both the character and design of the Creator as well as the creation itself—whether it is a celestial body, an herb, or an animal. All creation functioned in perfect harmony. None departed from its particular purpose. Sin, as we know it, had no sway over this perfect existence.

The biblical authors continually point back to God's creative work to provoke both awe and worship. According to Psalm 19, "The heavens declare the glory of God, and the sky above proclaims his handiwork." Also, Romans 1:20, "For his invisible attributes, namely, his eternal power and divine nature, have been clearly perceived, ever since the creation of the world, in the things that have been made." In other words, God's power, freedom, and goodness could be clearly seen in creation.

Much more could be said about the goodness of God's creation. But we must be careful to see how God's creation of animals and species of all kinds culminates in the creation of humanity, which He calls "very good."

Man: The Image of God

We encounter some peculiar language to describe the creation of mankind. Man and woman, complementary but distinct, are said to be "in our image, after our likeness" (Genesis 1:26). Unfortunately, the text does not spell out what this means. Yet it offers some evidence based on what God calls humanity to do:

1. Be fruitful and multiply
2. Subdue and have dominion

Man's calling says something about who he is. In other words, identity is related to purpose. Image-bearers cannot mean that we literally appear like God, because we have bodies and God doesn't. So there must be something deeper about our humanity.

When we consider these twin tasks as well as the testimony of the New Testament, we learn that the image of God in man means that we are rational beings, capable of communication and understanding, and moral beings, created in true righteousness and holiness. This image is *relational* because it means man is designed to relate to God in a way different from any other creature. He is unique because he has a conscience as a moral compass in light of true knowledge of God. Human beings are able, then, to carry out these two callings because they bear God's image. This picture is filled out a bit more by the fact that we've been created as embodied beings who have been given life by God's very breath, which is referred to as the spirit or soul (Genesis 1:30; 2:7). Because of our natural endowments as human creatures, we are capable of relationships with one another and with our Creator. We are also capable of fulfilling the cultural mandate, which concerns our fruitfulness and stewardship toward the earth. The creation, from this perspective, becomes a gift as opposed to a constraint or burden.

The Creator: Worthy of Worship

Many discussions about creation often overlook an important role that creation fulfills—that of pointing human beings to both the character of the Creator and the implications it has for worship. The question from finite human beings is obvious: "Why create?" After all, students of the Scriptures know that Genesis 3 occurs and human beings sink to incredible depths. They do not obey the will of God. Though the Bible never specifically answers this question, it does imply the answer in hints and shadows.

God is a self-sufficient being, so He was under no obligation to create. There was nothing lacking in His perfections that demanded it. He is free, operating under no external constraint. This means that there was something else that willed Him to create. The only other explanation that coheres with biblical truths is that God, being infinitely loving and gracious, decided to create in order to reveal something of His greatness and glory. This is certainly mind-boggling to consider. It even perhaps raises other questions. However, these are the types of questions that human beings, created to live in communion with their Creator, would ask. We are naturally overwhelmed by the reality that we happen to exist and are the objects of God's favor and eyewitnesses to His power. For Christians, worship is the only fitting response.

The psalmists are able expositors of God's greatness in creation. Hear their testimony:

> By the word of the Lord the heavens were made, and by the breath of his mouth all their host. He gathers the waters of the sea as a heap; he puts the deeps in storehouses. Let all the earth fear the Lord; let all the inhabitants of the world stand in awe of him! For he spoke, and it came to be; he commanded, and it stood firm.
>
> (Psalm 33:6-9)

> Let the heavens be glad, and let the earth rejoice; let the sea roar, and all that fills it; let the field exult, and everything in it!
>
> (Psalm 96:11-12a)

> Of old you laid the foundation of the earth, and the heavens are the work of your hands. They will perish, but you will remain; they will all wear out like a garment. You will change them like a robe, and they will pass away...
>
> (Psalm 102:25-26)

Other biblical writers also call human beings to worship in light of the Creator's handiwork:

> The LORD by wisdom founded the earth; by understanding he established the heavens.
>
> (Proverbs 3:19)

> Worthy are you, our Lord and God, to receive glory and honor and power, for you created all things, and by your will they existed and were created.
>
> (Revelation 4:11)

Evangelical Christians echo the sentiments of John Calvin, the great Protestant theologian and pastor. He called creation the theater of God's glory.[3] Yet within this grand theater, God is engaged in another important activity: providence.

Providence

Providence refers to the ways and means by which God sustains and governs the creation. While this definition is relatively straightforward, it is one intersection in Christian theology where various traditions part ways. Some emphasize God's providence in the area of the doctrine of salvation. They focus on how God brings sinners to salvation. Others tie the discussion of God's providence to the area of good and evil: how is it that God rules over a creation filled with such evil that taints His good creation? Still others treat providence as a euphemism for referring to a generic God that some believe just generally looks out for people according to His whims. While space doesn't permit us to try to address all of these complex matters nor to present all viewpoints, some general biblical observations are needed to bring clarity to this doctrine.

First, it is appropriate to discuss the subject of providence in conjunction with the doctrine of creation because the Christian God is an active, personal, living God. He does not spin creation into existence and then step back into shadowy darkness to watch it unwind. Instead, this is a God who cares about creation. He cares about birds and trees, tribes and nations. His loving concern is seen in the fact that He creates and later, as we learn, that He is a savior as well. Evangelical Christians agree that God and His heavenly agents (see chapter ten) are actively involved in earthly affairs.

Second, God is presented in Scripture as being crucial to the creation's stability. Colossians 1:17 specifically teaches that in Christ, God the Son, "all things hold together." Jesus Himself cautions us against anxiety because of the way God feeds even the birds (Matthew 6:26). Creation is sustained both in a larger cosmic sense, but also in the details of creation's provision. This is why God's promise to Noah in Genesis 8:22 is so important. He assures Noah and future generations of humankind that "while the earth remains, seedtime and harvest, cold and heat, summer and winter, day and night, shall not cease." This of course doesn't relieve human beings from their charge to faithful stewardship. It also doesn't preclude the possibility of inclement weather. What it does mean is that we can expect some regularity in creation because of God's sustaining promise.

Finally, God's will for the world and actions in it are always interwoven with the decisions of human agents. Many theologians and church traditions have differed on how this relationship between God's sovereign deeds and the actions of responsible human agents is to be constructed. However, there is largely a consensus throughout the Christian tradition that both God's character and power are not cancelled out by human decisions, nor is decision-making (whether to accept Christ or do evil) an insignificant part of human life.

One of the reasons this subject is so complex is because of what is to many the most perplexing riddle of existence: evil. Our understanding of the Christian doctrine of sin is best begun with the question, "What's wrong with the world?"

What's Wrong with the World?

When Americans are polled about what they believe is the most challenging issue facing their nation, they supply a plethora of responses. For some it is economic concerns, whether it be inflation, tax policies, or the national debt. Others point to the growing environmental crises and alternative energy needs. And yet there are always those who believe social and domestic issues, such as immigration policy, abortion, and marriage legislation should occupy our thoughts.

The irony of such answers is that despite their apparent diversity, there is a core concern that unites them. Whenever we carefully consider the source of these problems, as well as the forces that cause them to continue to plague human society, it ultimately comes back to what has happened to God's good creation. Theologians call it "the fall."

The Fall

Much ink has been spilled as experts in many academic disciplines and professional fields attempt to explain what is wrong with the world. Physicians know something is wrong; AIDS relief workers in sub-Saharan Africa know it; prison wardens know it; everyone knows it. How we answer the question, "What's wrong with the world?" is a pivotal cornerstone of a Christian worldview. For Christians, it all begins with the narrative of Genesis 3.

In Genesis 3, readers encounter an account of human beings dwelling in harmony in the Garden of Eden. This harmony is disrupted when one of God's creatures, a serpent to be exact, entices them. As we later learn in Scripture, Satan assumed the form of this creature in order to undermine something fundamental about God's relationship with mankind: obedience to His will. God made known His will to Adam and Eve in the same manner He does to us today—through His word. Our first parents, however, were privileged to verbally hear God's truth. But the simple question, "Did God really say that?" was the undoing of this beautiful existence enjoyed by God's creatures. Adam and Eve partook of a tree's fruits, which opened them to a way of seeing themselves, each other, and God that was contrary to their Creator's plan. Immediately their decision—a sin, to be exact—brought shame. In a moment, human disobedience ushered the creation into a brokenness God never desired for it.

Consequences of the Fall

Cornelius Plantinga has poignantly said, "The story of the fall tells us that sin corrupts: it puts asunder what God has joined together and joins together what God has put asunder."[4] This is seen very sharply in the events that immediately follow. Estrangement happened on a basic level between the man and woman because they could no longer dwell together in openness with their bodies. But this estrangement is demonstrated even more profoundly in how they relate to God: "And they heard the sound of the LORD God walking in the garden in the cool of the day, and the man and his wife hid themselves from the presence of the LORD God among the trees of the garden" (Genesis 3:8). When God inquires about their whereabouts, they identify the shame of their nakedness as their reason for hiding. But this only further exposes them. Their violation is uncovered as swiftly as their nakedness was once they tasted the tree's fruit. This first couple acknowledges the deception they fell prey to, and then God's judgment falls.

It is evident from the narrative that something about the communion God and humanity enjoyed has been lost. Yet the portrait becomes clearer as God announces judgment upon: (1) the serpent, (2) the woman, (3) the man, and (4) the earth itself. The serpent's judgment is marked by its place in the animal kingdom. The woman's judgment would come both in the form of her pain in childbirth and animosity toward her husband's leadership. Both of these are corruptions of human life that would have been free from complication apart from sin. The man's judgment would occur in his labors upon a cursed earth. Labor would go from joyful vocation to toilsome struggle. To add a final bookend to the severity of God's judgment, man and woman were expelled from the pristine garden.

The account of Genesis 3 has been hotly debated at times in Christian history, particularly the last two hundred years. Those who want to better understand the terms of this debate, especially concerning its historicity, should peruse the books recommended for further reading at the end of this chapter. However, it is of great importance for Christians to understand the implications of the fall beyond the Garden of Eden.

The taint of sin's presence and the consequences that follow has, like a genetic disease, made its way down humanity's family tree to our own time. We often associate this disease with specific sinful acts. After all, even unbelievers acknowledge "nobody's perfect." However, the origin of sin runs much deeper than mere deeds. As Henri Blocher puts it, "Alienation from God, the condition of being deprived and depraved, follows immediately upon the first act of sinning—for Adam himself and for his seed after him."[5] Adam, then, functions not only as a biological head of the human race, but also a spiritual forerunner. His nature is not unlike ours. Though human beings change over time, Adam and Eve were humans created in the image of God as we are today. Yet how they used the freedom of will God gave them had consequences that affected the whole person, and by extension, have affected all humankind.

In Ephesians 2:1-3, the Apostle Paul captures the human plight well as he recounts the spiritual biographies of Christians in the Ephesian church:

And you were dead in the trespasses and sins in which you once walked, following the course of this world, following the prince of the power of the air, the spirit that is now at work in the sons of disobedience—among whom we all once lived in the passions of our flesh, carrying out the desires of the body and the mind, and were by nature children of wrath, like the rest of mankind.

In order to understand this passage, we will need a clearer understanding of what sin is. The Bible uses an array of images, events, and terminology to describe the phenomenon we know as sin. In its simplest form, it means missing the mark. There is a moral standard God has erected for human beings to live by that they have failed to obtain. In this way, we can call sin a violation of God's law, which is an expression of His will for human beings. It also, of course, violates His character as a holy God. But sin is far more than this. As one theologian puts it, "Sin is not only the breaking of law but also the breaking of covenant with one's savior. Sin is the smearing of a relationship, the grieving of one's divine parent...a betrayal of the partner to whom one is joined by a holy bond."[6]

Seeing sin in relational terms is helpful because it puts our clear violation of God's laws into spiritual perspective. It isn't simply a legal matter. It is rebellion against the king of the universe. Yet it is also a child's rejection of a Father's compassionate embrace in order to pursue his own ends. Once again, Plantinga captures this point: "Let us say that a sin is any act—any thought, desire, emotion, word, or deed—or its particular absence, that displeases God and deserves blame."[7]

Now that we have a grasp of what sin is, we should return to Paul's words to the Ephesians. While in Genesis 3 we learn of a foe named Satan who targets Christian obedience, Paul suggests here that there are two spiritual reference points we should focus on when it comes to sin. The first is the world. He isn't referring to particular people or the planet earth. He is speaking about systems, authorities, values, and forces that stand in defiance of God. They are the by-products of a world in which human beings have distorted and corrupted so much of what is good and true. Worldliness, then, is a challenge to Christian faithfulness.

The second is the more specific root for the first: the flesh. Paul doesn't mean that our bodies are the real problem that keeps us from following God. He is referring to our sinful nature, or the evil desires that come from our nature inherited from Adam. Apart from Christ, people pursue their own wicked desires or passions as opposed to being led by the Spirit of God. This is why throughout the New Testament, it says that the flesh and Spirit are at war with one another. The question is, "Who will be our Master?"

So then the world and the flesh constitute two real problems for the Christian life. But they are coupled with two other serious problems: guilt and depravity. Because human beings commit sins, they, much like common criminals, rightfully stand under judgment. They are charged with unrighteousness by the Righteous Judge and have been found guilty. As the psalmist says in Psalm 14:3, "They have all turned aside; together they have become corrupt; there is none who does good, not even one." The sinful nature humans possess is depraved. This speaks not only to the evil they have committed, but also to their bent toward evil. Unfortunately, we cannot claim that we tend to do good when left on our own. We always lean toward our own desires and not those of God.

With these truths being the case, how is it that we make sense of a good creation broken by sin? Better yet, does God still have a plan for this warped world?

Creation and Fall: The Need for Rescue

When we consider just how deep the corruption and perversion of God's creation goes, it is easy to despair. After all, it seems to rule out the prospect of enjoying any aspect of culture and creation. It also seems to minimize the possible reversal of fortunes for human beings. Creation indicts human wickedness, such as in the book of Isaiah.[8] God responds to Job's questions and doubts with questions of His own that silence Job in light of the power and majesty of the Creator's works. Even the human conscience won't leave unbelievers alone because it convicts them apart from any special revelation like Scripture (Romans 2:12-16). The creation may continue to yield some of its intended fruits, but this is simply the common grace of God. It still stands under a curse, according to Scripture.

However, according to the second half of Ephesians 2, there is hope. The phrase "but God" in verse 4 signals that God is not finished with His creatures. As we eventually learn, God's plan of redemption not only includes human beings, but creation itself. More will be said about this in subsequent chapters. But some have gone as far as to call the Christian story "creation regained." An important pivot point in that story is Genesis 3:15: "I will put enmity between you and the woman, and between your offspring and her offspring; he shall bruise your head, and you shall bruise his heel." This verse, though somewhat cryptic, is an announcement of hope. Yet this hope is deeply veiled at this point in God's great redemptive story. In the next chapter of this book we will discover the true identity of the woman's seed. His name is Jesus.

For Further Reading:

Collins, C. John. *Did Adam and Eve Really Exist?: Who They Were and Why You Should Care*. Wheaton, IL: Crossway, 2011. **(I)**

Plantinga, Cornelius. *Not the Way It's Supposed to Be: A Breviary of Sin*. Grand Rapids, MI: Eerdmans, 1995. **(B)**

Wolters, Albert. *Creation Regained: Biblical Basics for a Reformational Worldview.* Grand Rapids, MI: Eerdmans, 1985. **(I)**

---

[1] Graham Cole, *God the Peacemaker: How Atonement Brings Shalom* (Downers Grove, IL: InterVarsity Press, 2009), 53.

[2] Norman Geisler and Frank Turek, *I Don't Have Enough Faith to Be an Atheist* (Wheaton, IL: Crossway, 2004), 73.

[3] John Calvin, *The Institutes of the Christian Religion*, 1.5.8.

[4] Cornelius Plantinga, Jr., *Not the Way It's Supposed to Be: A Breviary of Sin* (Grand Rapids, MI: Eerdmans, 1995), 30.

[5] Henri Blocher, *Original Sin: Illuminating the Riddle* (Downers Grove, IL: InterVarsity Press, 1997), 128.

[6] Plantinga, Jr., 12.

[7] Ibid., 13.

[8] Matthew Bracey, "A Gracious Hope: Isaiah's Biblical Theology of Creation," *Helwys Society Forum,* March 26, 2012, accessed August 17, 2012, http://www.helwyssocietyforum.com/?p=2041.

4

The Person and Work of Christ

As a matter of principle, we don't like being told how bad we are. We thrive on compliments, praise, and reward, not pessimism or critique. We prefer to hear and believe the best about ourselves. However, this tendency is further evidence of our fallen state. As we saw in chapter three, the human condition is a serious one. It is one that not only signals a diminished quality of life, but also an ultimate end to life because of sin. It is only because of the glimmers of hope in the Old Testament, such as a promised offspring (Genesis 3:15) and a new covenant (Jeremiah 31:31-34), that we look forward to something better.

God's response to cries of distress and despair is His own Son, the second person of the Trinity. It is this Son who takes on human flesh and is who we know as Jesus of Nazareth. The New Testament actually sharpens our understanding of His identity by calling Him the Christ—the Greek word for the Hebrew "Messiah," the anointed one of God. Who exactly is Jesus Christ? Why did He come? What did He accomplish? These are the specific concerns of chapter four.

Two important qualifications will be helpful to readers as they study this chapter: First, because Christ's person and work is connected with the salvation of sinners, readers should anticipate some similar themes here and in chapter six; second, because Christ is the Son of God, the second person of the Trinity, some of what is said here will be in reference to the Father and Spirit, who are also discussed in chapters two and five. So when taken as a unit, this section of the book seeks to present a coherent understanding of whom Christians believe God is and what this entails.

Prophet, Priest, and King

Historically, the Christian tradition has described Jesus as fulfilling a three-fold office of prophet, priest, and king. Robert Letham suggests that while Jesus may not have named Himself using these terms, they are useful because they are ascribed to Him by the biblical authors, and they also seem to represent the aims of Jesus' ministry, as seen from a practical vantage point.[1] This being the case, we'll proceed using them to better understand who Jesus is and what He did. At the same time, we'll walk through key events in the life of Jesus as these titles/offices are relevant and unveil the most radical truth about who Jesus is—fully God and fully man.

No Ordinary Birth

Jesus' birth was anything but ordinary. As far as controversy and modern thought go, it is an enormous stumbling block for many. The Bible teaches that a young virgin, engaged to an honorable Jewish man, was visited by an angel. But it isn't mere appearances that startle and shock—this young virgin would become the one spoken of in Isaiah 7:14; she would bear a child who would be called Immanuel ("God with us"). Matthew's Gospel clarifies any doubt the skeptic may have when it says that the news of Jesus' birth, delivered to both Joseph and Mary separately, fulfilled the words of the prophet Isaiah (Matthew 1:22-23).

Both Immanuel and Jesus are significant names. The first attests to Christ's oneness with God; the latter attests to His role as Savior or Deliverer (the Greek version of "Joshua"). Yet even the circumstances of Jesus' birth are revealing because they indicate something about His identity. He is certainly the Son of God, conceived by the Holy Spirit. But this child is a king. This is evidenced by two ironies in the Gospels. First, when Herod, king of Judea, heard about the birth of a so-called "king of the Jews," he secretly sought to have this child killed. Of course, God's angelic messengers intervened, curtailing his plans. Second, the wise men who came from the East to worship Jesus came bearing gifts—not unlike how one would approach a king. So although Jesus was a mere babe to some, many of the parties described in the early days of His life knew that He was so much more.

The theological language used by Christians throughout to describe Jesus' birth is "incarnation." Literally this means the taking on of flesh. The Son of God came to earth and carried out an earthly ministry. John's Gospel gives this important theological background in the prologue (1:1-4):

> In the beginning was the Word, and the Word was with God, and the Word was God. He was in the beginning with God. All things were made through him, and without him was not any thing made that was made. In him was life, and the life was the light of men.

It gradually becomes obvious that John means "Word" to refer to Jesus Christ. We are taught here that the man Jesus was also equal with God. There was never a time when He did not exist. This is why studies in Christology often include sections on the "pre-existence of Christ."[2] We want to avoid the error of so many in the earliest centuries of the Christian church, who either diminished Christ's humanity and emphasized His divinity, or who emphasized His humanity and diminished His divinity.

Raising a King

Interestingly, the Scriptures say very little about the time from Jesus' birth until the beginning of His public ministry. As if the remarkable circumstances of His birth weren't enough, Luke contributes two experiences from the childhood of Jesus that help us better understand His identity as the long-awaited Messiah.

First, when the appropriate time came for Jesus to be brought to the temple to be presented to the Lord, some curious spectators were already waiting for Him (Luke 2:22-38). Joseph and Mary first encounter a devout man named Simeon, who had been sustained by the Holy Spirit's promise: that he would not see death before he saw the Lord's Christ. So when Simeon's gaze fell upon Jesus, he raised Him in his arms, blessed God, and declared that he had seen God's salvation— one who would be a light to the nations and glory to Israel. Though Simeon's remarks startled the young couple, he was pointing to the powerful, transformative life that lay before young Jesus.

There is a second subtle event Luke records that, in a veiled way, points us both to Jesus' closeness with God and also the prophetic nature of His identity. Humorously, it occurs after Jesus' parents realize they have accidentally left their 12-year-old son behind after their annual trip to the temple. The frantic parents eventually return to the temple, and the sight is nothing short of incredible: their young son is in dialogue with the rabbis, causing them to marvel at His keen sense of understanding. This boy already has a sufficient handle on God's law to wow the teachers of His day. But it is His response to His upset mother's question that is most telling. When she asks why He has distressed them with His disappearance, He responds, "Why were you looking for me? Did you not know that I must be in my Father's house?" (Luke 2:49). This was enough to provoke questioning in the hearts of His parents, but it is enough to confirm our initial convictions about Christ: there is a close relationship between this Messiah and God. To God, this Jesus is a *son*.

An Unforgettable Baptism

While baptism is a historic, biblical practice that we will discuss later, it is interesting to think of it in reference to Christ. We learn from Him that it is more than a mere cultural practice unnecessarily perpetuated by some American churches; it is a meaningful act that was modeled by Christ.

Jesus' baptism signaled that He enjoyed a relationship with God the Father and God the Spirit in a way that transcends others:

> And when he came up out of the water, immediately he saw the heavens being torn open and the Spirit descending on him like a dove. And a voice came from heaven, "You are my beloved Son; with you I am well pleased."
>
> (Mark 1:10-11)

Jesus' identity is not only the Messiah of whom John the Baptist had been preaching. His Sonship is also plainly in view here. Additionally, the Spirit falling upon Him seemingly confirms His prophetic role. Of course, the word "Christ" means "anointed one." But in the Old Testament, we often see the Spirit of God come upon prophets and leaders when they are carrying out God's will (e.g., 1 Samuel 16:13). In other cases, the Scriptures note that the word of God came to a particular person (e.g., 1 Samuel 3:1-19). For Jewish onlookers and contemporary readers familiar with the Old Testament, this is difficult to overlook.

It is in John's account that our developing portrait is further clarified. When John the Baptist saw Jesus, he made a crucial statement: "Behold, the Lamb of God, who takes away the sin of the world!" (John 1:29). Jesus' identity as Messiah, Son of God, and messenger from God (prophet) is tied to His priestly work. After all, lambs are animals that are connected with the sacrificial system. They remind one of the Passover during which the blood of lambs spread over the Hebrew doorposts in Egypt preserved their firstborn sons (Exodus 12). In this, the blood of lambs, in some sense, covered the people prior to the institution of the Mosaic Covenant and formalized sacrificial system. This reference also reminds us of the priests who, on the Day of Atonement, would offer goats and bulls on behalf of the sins of the people (Leviticus 16). All of these details are a part of how the New Testament will put into perspective just what Jesus' death accomplished. According to the author of Hebrews, Jesus is not only a high priest who offers a once-and-for-all sacrifice for the sins of people, He is also the sacrifice Himself! Already in John 1 this is hinted at in John the Baptist's words.

Tempted and Tried

Before Jesus began His public ministry, He was driven by the Spirit into the wilderness to be tempted (Matthew 4:1-11; Mark 1:12-14; Luke 4:1-13). Satan comes to Jesus with three temptations. Two twist God's Word in an attempt to disrupt Jesus' perfect relationship with His heavenly Father, and another seeks to deliver the promise of glory and authority apart from God's plan for Christ's humiliation and, only later, exaltation.

Each of these would have betrayed Jesus' confidence in His Father's word and provision. Jesus instead demonstrated perfect obedience to and confidence in the will and word of the Father. And yet, His very priesthood for sinners is relevant to these temptations. According to Hebrews 2:17-18, Christ is able to be a merciful priest because He sympathizes with us in our temptations. Jesus' humanity is in view here since the high priests of old were chosen of men. Yet in these same verses, we are told that high priests are able "to make propitiation for the sins of the people." This means that the sacrifices made are able to, at least for a time, turn God's wrath away from them. However, the Levitical priesthood was never finally able to atone for sins and deliver people completely from God's wrath. Only a perfect sacrifice will do. Jesus is the only One able to propitiate for sins because only He Himself can satisfy the wrath of God.

What the temptation of the Son ultimately reminds us of is Jesus' wholehearted commitment to the reason for which the Father sent Him: to give His life as a ransom for many (Mark 10:45). It is this purpose that is embodied in the words He spoke and deeds He performed during His ministry.

Jesus Goes Public

Because Christians are called to share their faith with others, we tend to summarize the tenets of Christianity. Certainly there is a place for doctrinal statements and theology books. However, in speaking about the faith, we often present concise descriptions of what Jesus came to do: He came to save sinners. We often believe it to be overwhelming to explain every teaching, event, or parable in every conversation. While this is understandable, the practical downside is that we reduce the message of Christ to His death and resurrection, namely the cross. This then eclipses the powerful way Jesus' life attests to who He is. There are three features of Jesus' ministry that I will call attention to here: (1) His preaching of the kingdom; (2) His miraculous signs and deeds; and (3) His call to discipleship.

Preaching the Kingdom

The ministry of John the Baptist preceded Jesus' ministry. Many were tempted to ascribe more significance to him, but he only pointed them to the One about whom he preached. Once Jesus had been baptized and emerged onto the scene, He began teaching primarily in the synagogues (e.g., Luke 4:15). However, Mark's account most simply captures the theme that undergirded Jesus' ministry:

Now after John was arrested, Jesus came into Galilee, proclaiming the gospel of God, and saying, "The time is fulfilled, and the kingdom of God is at hand; repent and believe in the gospel."

(Mark 1:14-15)

For Jesus to preach this way is noticeable. First, for Jesus to preach following John the Baptist would, in some sense, make Him appear as a prophet. John knew Jesus was great, but there was no doubt people would think Him to be a prophet as they did John (John 1:21). And as we have already seen, Jesus did fulfill a prophetic role by coming and speaking for God. Yet He was not a prophet in the strict sense—the sense that the people of Israel were accustomed to.

Second, these verses are important because Jesus is inaugurating the kingdom of God. This provoked great interest among the people. The common man understands that you cannot have a kingdom without a king. So is Jesus a king? Is He, more specifically, the long-awaited Messiah? These are the sort of questions that caused great consternation for many in Jesus' day.

Finally, this message is notable because God's kingdom being at hand is evidently good news. After all, the word "gospel" means just that—"good news." However, this is not exactly how many received this news. One day, Jesus entered a synagogue on the Sabbath and read the following passage from Isaiah:

The Spirit of the Lord is upon me, because he has anointed me to proclaim good news to the poor. He has sent me to proclaim liberty to the captives and recovering of sight to the blind, to set at liberty those who are oppressed, to proclaim the year of the Lord's favor.

(Luke 4:18-19, quoting Isaiah 61:1-2a)

It was this passage, coupled with Jesus' next statement, which startled the people: "Today this Scripture has been fulfilled in your hearing." Jesus elicited great anger from people when He spoke of Himself alongside such prophets as Elijah and Elisha. They weren't prepared to hear a gospel that involved repentance, or one that included people besides Jews. But Jesus came announcing a kingdom that would come to fruition through His own life, death, resurrection, and return.

Miraculous Signs and Deeds

Miraculous signs and deeds accompanied Christ's ministry. He fed thousands from meager portions. He gave sight to the blind. He even raised a few individuals from the dead. Volumes could and have been written cataloguing and explaining these. For a general outlook on miracles, C. S. Lewis' *Miracles* is still a classic worth perusing. However, there are two chief considerations here.

First, Jesus' signs and deeds demonstrated divine power and authority. This is why the blind man whose sight was restored marveled at the Pharisees' unwillingness to believe that Jesus healed him. It was clear to him that there was something different and mighty about this man. Yet the religious leaders couldn't fathom that someone they despised could demonstrate such power in healing (John 9). In another instance, Jesus' raising of Lazarus from the dead was an occasion for Him to declare, "I am the resurrection and the life. Whoever believes in me, though he die, yet shall he live" (John 11:25). Jesus' raising of Lazarus and promise of life to others clearly showed what John intended his Gospel to accomplish: "These [things] are written so that you may believe that Jesus is the Christ, the Son of God, and that by believing you may have life in his name" (John 20:31).

Second, interwoven with these displays of power were opportunities for Jesus to unveil deeper spiritual realities. Jesus' signs and deeds were intended to partially fulfill the promise of Isaiah 61:1-3, which foretold of One who would not only preach, but also bring healing, restoration, liberation, and comfort. Specifically, His ministry was a foretaste of His kingdom when it came in its fullness at His second coming. This point will be expanded upon in chapter twelve.

The Call to Discipleship

Jesus could have assumed some earthly throne or office to spread His kingdom message. For that matter, He could have made use of His miracle-working power to write it in the sky so it would be unmistakable. However, Christ used twelve ordinary men to change the world.

When Jesus called disciples, He was actually continuing a pattern begun by God when He made a covenant with Abraham (Genesis 12:1-3). God has always had a people set apart for His special purposes in the world. In Jesus, that covenant would include peoples from every tribe, tongue, and nation. Yet Jesus involved people in the work that He was doing (and He still does today!). Jesus wasn't a loner or hermit. He shared life with twelve followers. These disciples would come to be known as apostles—those commissioned specifically by the Lord Jesus. He explained the meaning of His parables to them. He even washed their feet. Yet they doubted, disagreed, and even deserted Jesus when He was arrested. How could King Jesus use such subjects in His kingdom?

The truth is that the call to discipleship comes to all Christians. This is clear from the Great Commission:

> All authority in heaven and on earth has been given to me. Go therefore and make disciples of all nations, baptizing them in the name of the Father and of the Son and of the Holy Spirit, teaching them to observe all that I have commanded you. And behold, I am with you always, to the end of the age.
>
> (Matthew 28:18-20)

Jesus, then, is calling all people to salvation. He is calling them to be His disciples of the Trinitarian God we learned about in chapter two. While more of the implications of this call will be explained in later chapters, for now we should recognize that Jesus is creating a new community through His ministry. He is calling people to become citizens of a different kind of kingdom, one where He is Savior and King.

On the Cross, In Our Place

The incarnation is often linked with another aspect of Jesus' work—His humiliation. This is what Paul speaks of in Philippians 2:5-8:

> Have this mind among yourselves, which is yours in Christ Jesus, who, though he was in the form of God, did not count equality with God a thing to be grasped, but emptied himself, by taking the form of a servant, being born in the likeness of men. And being found in human form, he humbled himself by becoming obedient to the point of death, even death on a cross.

The Apostle Paul is demonstrating that Christ did not cling to His divinity so He would not condescend to our lowly, human estate. No, Jesus came to us. And as He was arrested, tried, and slain on the cross, the depth of His love was on display for all to see.

Unfortunately, even in the midst of His death, many were not yet able to see this love. Luke does recount that one of the two thieves crucified on either side of Jesus trusted in Christ for salvation (Luke 23:42-43). Matthew also tells of a centurion who witnessed the earthquake and other astounding events that accompanied Jesus' death and was persuaded: "Truly this was the Son of God!" (Matthew 27:54). However, it is astonishing how few of those complicit in Jesus' death understood their actions. They didn't recognize the irony of the inscription posted above Him on the cross: "This is the King of the Jews" (Luke 23:38).

Who was responsible for the death of Jesus? Any unbiased reader would want to know, for it is obvious that Jesus was sinless (e.g., Matthew 3:15; Hebrews 4:15). A first party to indict would be God since He sent the Son to die for the sins of the whole world (cf. John 3:16). But it certainly appears that the chief priests, scribes, and elders were responsible, too. John Stott helpfully points out that it is important we keep both these truths in hand, despite the apparent tension:

> On the human level, Judas gave [Jesus] up to the priests, who gave him up to Pilate, who gave him up to the soldiers, who crucified him. But on the divine level, the Father gave him up, and he gave himself up, to die for us...he did not die; he was killed. Now, however, I have to balance this answer with its opposite. He was not killed; he died, giving himself up voluntarily to do his Father's will.[3]

The Apostle Paul summarizes the matter further by explaining to the Corinthians what God was doing in Christ:

> In Christ God was reconciling the world to himself, not counting their trespasses against them, and entrusting to us the message of reconciliation....For our sake he made him to be sin who knew no sin, so that in him we might become the righteousness of God.

> (2 Corinthians 5:19, 21)

The point, then, is to see that the people who killed Jesus rejected Him since He came with a message that exposed the darkness of the human heart and offered a remedy they would not accept. But it was in His sacrificial death that He fulfilled the will of the Father, accepting the penalty for sinners in their stead.

Yet how does one know if His sacrifice was accepted? How do we know that guilt, sin, and death itself have been dealt with? The answers to these questions are found in an empty tomb.

The Empty Tomb

Conversations about Christ's resurrection often shift quickly to apologetics. The resurrection, then, becomes a subject for historical investigation in order to silence the skeptics. Obviously there is a need for this type of exercise. In fact, the Apostle Paul began his discussion of the matter with the Corinthian church by attesting to the evidence of Christ's resurrection (1 Corinthians 15:3-8). However, we want to keep with the basic storyline we have been following in which we see Jesus emerge as a prophet, priest, and king.

Jesus' priesthood is not isolated to His work on the cross. After all, what if He stayed dead? How could we affirm He offered an acceptable sacrifice to God? Better yet, in what sense could we say He was truly God and truly man if death held Him as it will our mortal bodies one day? The tensions these questions create are many, but they are resolved by the startling discovery of Jesus' followers, as well as the post-resurrection appearances to many.

Many have attempted to dismiss the resurrection. Some call the resurrection a mental projection of emotionally distraught people. A few describe the event as a "spiritual resurrection" but not a bodily one. Others go so far as to say Jesus never really died! All of these accounts not only clash with the details found in the Gospels, they also defy much of the recent scholarship done by biblical scholars of various theological traditions. One can refer to the recommended readings at the end of this chapter to better understand the historical and scientific objections.

For our purposes, we need only to understand that historic Christianity has always affirmed that Jesus' resurrection was a bodily resurrection. It signaled His triumph over death, sin, and the forces of Satan. It meant that the Father accepted His sacrifice and raised Him bodily as a sign that He was not done with creation. God, in fact, was affirming the goodness of the body and the material world. To use scriptural language, Christ's resurrection was the "firstfruits" of our future resurrection (1 Corinthians 15:20). More will be said on this later, but to discard this part of the story is to cast doubt on the rest. To believe that God created the world, that Christ performed miracles, and then to doubt the resurrection of Christ is to render a person inconsistent. Either Jesus was lying when He said He would rise again, or He was not (e.g., Mark 8:31). There is no middle ground.

Risen and Coming Again

Confidence in Christ's second coming has, in many quarters, fallen on hard times. Some suggest that His coming kingdom is something the Christian church ushers in through its faithful ministry. However, we are cautioned by the Apostle Peter that in the last days—the time between Christ's first and second coming—scoffers will say, "Where is the promise of his coming?" (2 Peter 3:4). Therefore, it is a belief that faithful believers must hold intact.

The first reason for confidence in the second coming is that it is plainly scriptural. For example, in Acts 1, Jesus' apostles have been left with a command to go to the nations with the message of Christ. And yet following His ascension, they are embarrassed by the angels who urge them to get to the task at hand as they stare into heaven. They warn, "This Jesus, who was taken up from you into heaven, will come in the same way as you saw him go into heaven" (Acts 1:11). This leaves little room for doubt, since angels are God's very messengers (see chapter ten).

The second reason Christians believe that Christ will come again is that the New Testament grounds Christian hope in both the resurrection as well as this event. Christians have good reason to believe in the first but are often tempted to doubt the second. The earliest disciples faced extreme persecution and hardship as a direct result of knowing Christ. Among the virtues God's Spirit produced in them was hope (e.g., 1 Corinthians 13:13; Galatians 5:5). Christians are hopeful because when Christ returns, the presence of sin will be completely removed. Sorrow will be no more. Death's stinger will be plucked free from our bodies. And those believers who have already experienced death will be raised to new life (e.g., 1 Corinthians 15:12-19). So, then, the second coming is no mere legend; it is part and parcel of historic Christianity.

Who Do You Say that I Am?

Every major religion offers some perspective on Jesus. What many Christians may be surprised to learn is that most of these other faiths offer somewhat positive portraits of Jesus. In the case of Islam, Jesus is seen as a great prophet. Yet Muslims do not believe He actually died on the cross. To offer another perspective, faiths such as Mormonism seemingly espouse many traditional Christian teachings but upon closer inspection, adopt a different perspective on Jesus' eternality with the Father. Jesus' question to His disciples, "Who do you say that I am?" is just as pertinent to us now as it was in the first century.

Jesus is indeed a prophet, but not like Jeremiah or Habakkuk. This prophet came bearing the fullest and final revelation of God: Himself (Hebrews 1:1-4). And for this testimony, He was crucified, having been treated as a false prophet and blasphemer (e.g., Matthew 26:65; Luke 22:64). Jesus is also a priest, though not from the tribe of Levi. At first glance, this is contrary to biblical law. However, Scripture reminds us that this priest is greater than the rest—He actually comes from the line of Melchizedek, not Aaron (Hebrews 5:10). However, for all the mystery surrounding this shadowy Old Testament figure, Melchizedek was not only a priest but also a king (Genesis 14:18). Jesus became a servant so we might be set free, so it is difficult to appreciate His kingship. However, His resurrection and commission to go to the nations with His Gospel settles the matter. Yet we do not go alone. The Comforter, the Holy Spirit, goes with us. It is this person of the Trinity we turn to in chapter five.

For Further Reading:

Lewis, C. S. *Miracles.* New York: HarperOne, 2001. **(I)**

Moore, Russell D. *Tempted and Tried: Temptation and the Triumph of Christ.* Wheaton, IL: Crossway, 2011. **(B)**

Stott, John R. W. *The Cross of Christ.* Downers Grove, IL: InterVarsity Press, 1986. **(I)**

Wright, N. T *The Resurrection of the Son of God.* Minneapolis: Fortress Press, 2003. **(A)**

---

[1] Robert Letham, *The Work of Christ* (Downers Grove, IL: InterVarsity Press, 1993), 19-20.

[2] Donald Macleod, *The Person of Christ* (Downers Grove, IL: InterVarsity Press, 1998), 45-70.

[3] John R. W. Stott, *The Cross of Christ* (Downers Grove, IL: InterVarsity Press, 1986), 64-65.

5

The Person and Work of the Holy Spirit

The Christian God is one that perplexes followers of other religions. He is one of great love and mercy, yet also one who punishes the wicked. He inspires awe and worship because of His infinite power, and yet He can also be approached in prayer. But the most unique truth about Him, as we learned earlier, is that He is a Trinitarian God. He externally exists in three persons: Father, Son, and Holy Spirit.

We've briefly considered the character and work of God from the overall message of Scripture. Usually when we speak of Him, we are often thinking particularly about God the Father. Yet the very same attributes are evident in the person and work of Jesus Christ, the incarnate Son. Though He is one in His essence with the Godhead, He is a distinct person, to use the language of the Christian tradition. In salvation, He operates as the most visible agent of our redemption because He comes as a man. However, there is a third member of the Trinity who is equal in power, glory, and honor: the Holy Spirit.

Who is the Holy Spirit, or the Holy Ghost as some Bible translations put it? What does He do? What does Scripture teach about His person and work? In this chapter, we'll explore the foundations of this important doctrine. In the next chapter, the Holy Spirit's work in salvation will be explained. Then in chapter seven, we'll consider the nature of that work once one has become a Christian.

Initial Considerations

There are two primary obstacles that Christians encounter when understanding what the Bible teaches about the Holy Spirit. The first obstacle has to do with language itself. The terminology in both Hebrew (*ruach/nephesh*) and Greek (*pneuma*) has a fairly wide range of meaning across the pages of Scripture.[1] For instance, *ruach* can simply mean "wind" or "breath." It is the word used in Genesis 1:2 when it says God created the heavens and the earth, and the Spirit of God was hovering over the face of the waters. When the words "God" or "Holy" are used in conjunction with the Spirit, something more than simple breath is meant. This is why context in interpretation is so important. Words have a range of meaning. In English, for instance, the word "sharp" has a semantic range. We use it to describe the quality of a knife in a kitchen drawer. It is also used to describe the intelligence of a person. It can even be used to describe how well someone dresses! In this same way, the language of "spirit" means different things in the Bible according to the context in which it occurs. This leads to the second difficulty in understanding the Holy Spirit: His person and work is gradually unfolded over the course of Scripture. How the Scriptures speak about Jesus Christ is similar. There are hints and shadows of this coming Messiah that are only finally unveiled in the New Testament. While the person of the Spirit never changes, the way He works in and among God's people is distinct from one Testament to the other.

Before we briefly survey this story of the Holy Spirit, an important qualification is needed. Because the identity of the Spirit is slowly unraveled from Genesis to Revelation (especially in Acts and the time of the early church), one might be inclined to believe that the Holy Spirit is a particular manifestation of God for that particular epoch of time. Yet by believing this, we can unintentionally distort the true nature of God. The Bible doesn't teach that the Son or Spirit were later manifestations of God or versions in which God existed. To teach this would be to fall prey to some version of modalism, an early false teaching that has been called heretical since the earliest church councils. Instead, the Scriptures paint a portrait of all three members of the Godhead—Father, Son, and Spirit—at work in the world, never divided in character or purposes, to bring about the redemption of the creation.

The Spirit from the Old Testament to the New

The Spirit of God is portrayed as being operative in several arenas. First, His role in creation is taught (e.g., Genesis 1:2). The Holy Spirit, like the Son, must not be thought of as a secondary created agent, as some have argued in the past. He existed eternally with the Father and the Son, and was active in the work of creation.

The Holy Spirit is also seen in various forms of leadership that occurred throughout the history of God's people. The Spirit who is upon Moses is also laid upon 70 elders in Numbers 11:16-30, enabling them to assist him in governing the people. The presence of God is also said to be with Samuel in his leadership, and particularly in reference to the way he handled God's Word (1 Samuel 2:21b; 3:19-21). The Spirit later would actually come upon Saul during his reign as king, empowering him for mighty deeds. However, he would ultimately disobey God, and the Spirit would depart and be replaced by an evil spirit (1 Samuel 11:6; 16:14). We begin to notice at this point that there is a very close relationship between the presence and work of the Spirit and the presence and work of God's Word. The two become practically inseparable as one journeys through the pages of Scripture.

Another aspect of biblical leadership where its relationship to the Spirit can be glimpsed is the practice of anointing, and later in the laying on of hands. While these were symbolic gestures, they are intended to convey something of God's own appointment as well as the presence of His Spirit (e.g., 1 Samuel 10:1). The anointing as well as the laying on of hands are still practices perpetuated by many evangelical traditions today. The laying on of hands is particularly seen in ordination customs (e.g., 2 Timothy 1:6-7).

The realm of prophecy is certainly one where the Spirit is active. Prophecy is, in some instances, a matter of foretelling. It is true that some upon whom God's Spirit rested could predict things to come. But a more precise way of describing this activity would be to call it "forth-telling." After all, the prophets were simply relaying in many cases the judgment God warned of in His covenants for those who departed from His law. This is where the Spirit's work of inspiration can be glimpsed. Not only do visions, oracles, and dreams represent God's divine call to and movement upon the prophets, but they hint at what the New Testament will teach concerning the inspiration of the Scriptures. Second Timothy 3:16, as we've already seen, teaches that "all Scripture is given by inspiration of God" (KJV). Literally, they are "God-breathed." Then the Apostle Peter unequivocally says that the prophets "spoke from God as they were carried along by the Holy Spirit" (2 Peter 1:21b). Again, the connection between the Word and Spirit is unmistakably clear. If fallen, sinful human beings are going to be capable of rightly portraying God's will in the form of His Word, they will need divine leadership for those prophetic tasks.

The giving of gifts is another role of the Spirit that is also related to leadership and prophecy. This theme appears in both Testaments. As early as Genesis, we learn of a young man named Joseph. While he undoubtedly had his faults, he finds himself in difficult circumstances because of his brothers' hatred toward him. However, God brings him into favor with the Pharaoh in Egypt because of his ability to interpret dreams (Genesis 41). Later, this same gift will be used by Daniel, another servant of God, which will prove to be quite useful and timely

(Daniel 2). The Spirit gives gifts that also empower individuals to construct the tabernacle. Specifically, Bezalel is said to have been filled "with the Spirit of God, with ability and intelligence, with knowledge and all craftsmanship" (Exodus 31:3). Later, as we move into the New Testament era, God gives the church "spiritual gifts" for carrying out the work of ministry. These gifts come to those who are united to Christ. While 1 Corinthians 12–14 speaks most extensively about spiritual gifts, it is mainly intended to serve as a corrective for a church abusing the gifts the Spirit had given. Although much more will be said later concerning conversion and the subsequent work of the Spirit, it is important to note that being in fellowship with the Holy Spirit has two dimensions: "The Spirit is given by the Father (Luke 11:13). But [He] is also *received* by the individual (John 7:39; Acts 19:2; Romans 8:15; Galatians 3:2)."[2]

It is worth noting that some of the references to God's Spirit in the Old Testament occasionally refer not so much to the Holy Spirit as we know Him from the New Testament record, but to the power or mind of God in a particular situation. In other words, every usage of "the Spirit of God" isn't exactly equivalent to "the Holy Spirit." This again speaks to the range of meaning that particular words can have *besides* simply "spirit." Yet this nuanced issue in biblical terminology need not trouble Christian readers. A helpful step in biblical interpretation (hermeneutics) concerning the Spirit is to observe how the New Testament builds bridges to the Old. A good example of this is found in 1 Peter 1:10-12:

> Concerning this salvation, the prophets who prophesied about
> the grace that was to be yours searched and inquired careful-
> ly, inquiring what person or time the Spirit of Christ in them
> was indicating when he predicted the sufferings of Christ and
> the subsequent glories. It was revealed to them that they were
> serving not themselves but you, in the things that have now been
> announced to you through those who preached the good news to
> you by the Holy Spirit sent from heaven, things into which angels
> long to look.

While this passage doesn't resolve every dilemma in discerning the Holy Spirit, it does demonstrate an important continuity between the activities of the Spirit in the Old Testament and how this is the same Spirit that Christians know and experience today. The Spirit-led prophets conveyed a faithful account of the Gospel that has now been realized and is preached today through the power of the Spirit from Scriptures inspired by the Spirit. Some of the other passages we will later consider also help us understand this relationship.

For some, the challenge of understanding the Holy Spirit has to do with His oneness with God. Language like "spirit" or "ghost" is not a typical part of our daily conversation; it remains locked in the realm of mystery for many. But it is when we see the Spirit's participation in the life of Christ that the inseparable link between Father, Son, and Spirit becomes transparent.

The Spirit in the
Life of Christ

The Holy Spirit's activity is by no means limited to a series of extraordinary events among God's prophets and peoples in the Old Testament. Both the new covenant of which Jeremiah speaks (cf. Jeremiah 31:31-34) and the message of Joel break forth in important demonstrations of power and divine activity in the New Testament. However, it is the Son whose birth, life, and victorious resurrection signal that God's Spirit—that is, the Holy Spirit—is present with Him.

The virginal conception of Christ is the most immediate demonstration that the Son and Spirit are no abstract or alien forces. First, Mary is told by the angel Gabriel who visits her that the circumstances of her child's birth will be unique. When she asks how she will conceive since she is a virgin, Gabriel responds, "The Holy Spirit will come upon you, and the power of the Most High will overshadow you; therefore the child to be born will be called holy—the Son of God" (Luke 1:35). The Holy Spirit, then, becomes the divine agent in the Son's incarnation.

At Jesus' baptism, this relationship is further developed. As we saw in chapter four, when Jesus is baptized, two remarkable things occur: First, the Spirit descends like a dove from heaven; and second, the voice of the Father breaks forth and declares Jesus to be His beloved Son (e.g., Mark 1:10). Arguably, there is never a clearer sign of the Trinitarian nature of the Godhead. This relationship between Father, Son, and Spirit is further explained concerning the childhood of Christ:

> There shall come forth a shoot from the stump of Jesse,
>   and a branch from his roots shall bear fruit.
> And the Spirit of the LORD shall rest upon him,
>   the Spirit of wisdom and understanding,
>   the Spirit of counsel and might,
>   the Spirit of knowledge and the fear of the LORD.
> And his delight shall be in the fear of the LORD.

> (Isaiah 11:1-3a)

Whether it is Jesus' baptism, His temptations, or the events of His ministry, Isaiah's prophecy seems to be fully embodied in the story of the Spirit. He accompanies Jesus from the very beginning until He is raised from the dead following His crucifixion. As the apostles would later preach, "God anointed Jesus of Nazareth with the Holy Spirit and with power" (Acts 10:38a). Jesus' ministry, then, becomes a snapshot of what it ideally looks like when a Christian is walking in the Spirit—a phrase that the New Testament writers are fond of using.

It is Jesus' final words to His disciples in John 14–17 that give greater insight into this.

John's Gospel enables us to see the Holy Spirit from a unique angle. Though He is mentioned long before John 14, it is in this important chapter that His identity is mentioned in the most explicit way. Jesus tells His wary disciples that if they would ask the Father, He would give them another Helper to be with them forever. This "Spirit of truth" would be unique to Christ-followers, and would dwell with them and in them (John 14:16-17). Some translations render Him as the Helper, while others the Comforter. I prefer "Helper" because it more broadly captures the breadth of all the Spirit does. He will instruct these forgetful, spiritually weary disciples (John 15:15; 16:13-15). He would reprove or correct the world concerning sin, righteousness, and judgment (John 16:7-11). This Spirit would do a work in the hearts of men that the Law was unable to do (more on this in chapter six).

The Bible has much to say about the Spirit's work in Christians today. However, it also says many intriguing things about His work among the earliest Christians following the ascension of Christ. It is to the crucial events of the earliest Christians that we now turn.

The Spirit and the
People of God

There was already evidence in the Old Testament that God's Spirit had a great work to do among His people. While the prophets present us with a number of striking and confusing images, one scene from a little-known prophet speaks to the coming work of the Spirit:

> And it shall come to pass afterward,
>   that I will pour out my Spirit on all flesh;
> your sons and your daughters shall prophesy,
>   your old men shall dream dreams,
>   and your young men shall see visions.
> Even on the male and female servants
>   in those days I will pour out my Spirit.

And I will show wonders in the heavens and on the earth, blood and fire and columns of smoke. The sun shall be turned to darkness, and the moon to blood, before the great and awesome day of the LORD comes. And it shall come to pass that everyone who calls on the name of the LORD shall be saved. For in Mount Zion and in Jerusalem there shall be those who escape, as the LORD has said, and among the survivors shall be those whom the LORD calls.

(Joel 2:28-32)

Many Jews who read this passage might have had difficulty making sense of it—especially prior to what occurred in Acts 2—but at Pentecost, people begin to understand.

Pentecost

After Jesus' resurrection and prior to His ascension, He gave His disciples instructions to wait in Jerusalem because soon they would be baptized with the Holy Spirit (Luke 24:49; Acts 1:4-5). The Old Testament had foretold that "in the last days the Spirit would be poured out—on the Servant Messiah (Isaiah 42:1), on Israel (Ezekiel 37:14), and on all the people (Joel 2:28-32)."[3] It was no coincidence that this outpouring of the Spirit would occur at the time of the Jewish feast known as Pentecost. This day bore great significance for the children of Abraham. It conveyed that God wasn't done with them yet, and that other nations would be included in God's gracious covenant.

The events of Acts 2 still perplex many because the outpouring of the Spirit was signaled by a mighty rushing wind followed by tongues like fire resting upon those present in Jerusalem. Yet it is the result that shocked the Jews and Gentiles alike: they were somehow able to hear one another speak in their respective languages! Some biblical scholars have noted that this passage has theological significance because it signals a great reversal begun by the Spirit. At Babel, God confounded human language as a part of His judgment against human rebellion (Genesis 11). However, in Acts 2, the work of God through the Spirit signals that new life and a future hope of renewal awaits the entire cosmos, starting with individuals who trust in Christ by faith. Thankfully, the Apostle Peter was present to place this extraordinary event in its proper perspective. Quoting from Joel 2, he helped the people make sense of how the Gospel had come to fruition in the outpouring of God's Spirit.

To the Ends of the Earth

While much more will be said about the Holy Spirit and the church later, we conclude our consideration of the Spirit's work by thinking about the important theme of *mission*. This theme is embodied in the Great Commission we considered earlier. But even prior to Pentecost, Jesus made a clear connection between His mission and the Spirit's empowerment: "But you will receive power when the Holy Spirit has come upon you, and you will be my witnesses in Jerusalem and in all Judea and Samaria, and to the end of the earth" (Acts 1:8).

This verse has launched countless mission agencies, shaped numerous evangelical efforts, and has motivated individual Christians to take the Gospel all over the world for centuries. The Holy Spirit, in other words, doesn't stop His work in Acts 2. He changes the lives of Christians through conversion and spiritual maturity. But the Spirit of God actually forms a community of believers with the purpose of being on a mission with God. From the earliest apostolic message to the present day, God's Word and His Spirit have enabled His people to be witnesses to His grace for His glory. As Peter and John stated boldly, "There is no other name under heaven given among men by which we must be saved" (Acts 4:12). Christopher Wright helpfully explains that "the phrase *under heaven* echoes the roll call of nations at Pentecost and indicates the universal claim that is being made."[4] The Spirit is then able to open the eyes of the spiritually blind, regardless of where they may be.

Conclusion

Spiritual guidance is one of the most important roles of the Holy Spirit in the Christian life. The reason for this is that the Bible teaches we must "test the spirits" because there are many who deceive (1 John 4:1-3). As we will see in later chapters, there are spirits who aren't from God. It isn't the human spirit necessarily that is in view here—though false teachers are indeed persons. It is those of the demonic realm who parade as the Spirit of truth when in fact they are from the father of lies—Satan. This is why it is so important to have a biblical pneumatology to guide our thoughts about the Holy Spirit and, in turn, to shape our practices in the Christian life.

For Further Reading:

Ferguson, Sinclair. *The Holy Spirit*. Downers Grove, IL: InterVarsity Press, 1996. **(I)**

Grudem, Wayne. *Systematic Theology: An Introduction to Biblical Doctrine*. Grand Rapids, MI: Zondervan, 2000 (specifically pages 635-653). **(B)**

Owen, John. *The Holy Spirit: His Gifts and Power*. Grand Rapids, MI: Kregel, 1954. **(I)**

[1] The study of the Holy Spirit is typically called "pneumatology," which stems from the Greek word typically translated as "spirit."

[2] Sinclair Ferguson, *The Holy Spirit* (Downers Grove, IL: InterVarsity Press, 1996), 92.

[3] Craig Bartholomew and Michael Goheen, *The Drama of Scripture: Finding Our Place in the Biblical Story* (Grand Rapids, MI: Baker Academic, 2004), 174.

[4] Christopher J. H. Wright, *The Mission of God: Unlocking the Bible's Grand Narrative* (Downers Grove, IL: IVP Academic, 2006), 515.

6

The Doctrine of Salvation

What must I do to be saved?" These were the words of a trembling jailer to Paul and Silas when they halted his suicide attempt in Acts 16. The jailer was simply responding in fear after a divinely sent earthquake opened the doors of jail cells and loosened shackles, freeing the prisoners for whom he was responsible. His well-timed question introduces our seventh biblical belief: the doctrine of salvation.

The study of salvation (also called soteriology) is as broad and rich as any other. There are many parts in Scripture that comprise the evangelical perspective on salvation. These parts are explained differently in various Protestant traditions. This being the case, some denominations will naturally stress some aspects of salvation more than others. A Lutheran will likely say more about justification, whereas a Presbyterian may say more about predestination or election. Even more, a Baptist may perhaps emphasize being born again (regeneration). The challenge for evangelical Christians is to have a basic understanding of what the Bible says on these matters, emphasizing what it teaches as fundamental to the doctrine of salvation. This is how we shall proceed in this chapter.

The Great Theme of Scripture

Because the Bible is both a powerful, influential book as well as a diverse book, many different emphases emerge from Genesis to Revelation. One of the temptations for those interpreting and explaining the Scripture is to reduce the biblical message to one theme over and against another. Christians in the scientific community will be tempted to represent the faith in a way that reduces it to a book about origins. Does the Bible address such issues? Absolutely. However, there is still more to the faith than this. Christians who are teachers or professors of literature may be inclined to only offer the scriptural message as one of aesthetic and literary beauty to admire. Certainly the Bible is an incredible achievement in terms of its diversity and unity, but it is more than mere literature. Finally, historically minded Christians might emphasize the narratives of the Old and New Testaments that bear the marks of parallel accounts by secular historians. Of course, God has acted in time and space. This means that we shouldn't be surprised at the unfolding of those deeds in Scripture. Yet despite all these important features of Scripture, we must recognize that they all point to a fundamental truth about the Bible: it is a book about salvation.

For those beginning to wrestle with and delve into the pages of Scripture, a helpful principle for interpretation can be to evaluate each text, character, or event in light of the fact that *God is saving a people.* This is seen clearly, for instance, in the account of the flood (Genesis 6–9), the flight of the Hebrews from Egypt (Exodus 3–12), and the return of the Jews from exile (Ezra—Nehemiah). So it is appropriate here to acknowledge that while salvation is something God does in the lives of individuals, it is always in reference to His plan to save peoples, nations, tribes, and tongues (e.g., Matthew 28:18-20).

Some readers may wonder why salvation appears as late as chapter six of this book if it comprises the overall message of Scripture. There are, in fact, important reasons why a book on Christian doctrine must begin with an account of creation and the fall before the subject of salvation. To be saved presupposes that there is some danger, risk, and even calamity from which someone needs to be saved. This is why understanding the fall is so important. But it is equally important to consider creation as it was in the beginning because it shows us the kindness and benevolence of God—the One who does not give up on human beings. It also helps us to better understand what God might be saving us *for*. In this chapter, we'll consider the necessity, grounds, condition, and immediate results of salvation. In doing this, we will be able to unite our voices with the words of one Presbyterian theologian who cites Jonah's words in surmising the Scriptures: "Salvation belongs to the LORD!" (Jonah 2:9).

The Necessity of Salvation

When considering the necessity of salvation, we should remember three important adjectives that capture an evangelical perspective: Universal, Exclusive, and Sufficient. Each of these taken out of this discussion can create confusion, but together they summarize the biblical account.

Universal

One aspect of 21st-century America that is not unlike the experience of the earliest apostles is that we live in a diverse culture. Our country has often been described as a melting pot of ethnicities, nationalities, and language groups, yet each group possesses its own ideas and customs. This means that we increasingly find ourselves in an environment where many worldviews compete for their share of the market in the public square. Some sound more plausible than others, but every individual will either adopt a position or will be gradually converted through the subtle force of social and spiritual influence. Despite the differences among religious options, Christianity teaches that all of humanity has the same fundamental need: to be reconciled to God. Regardless of any felt need that a person has or what their particular creed may say, the Scriptures declare "all have sinned and fall short of the glory of God" (Romans 3:23). This familiar verse follows another important teaching: "None is righteous, no, not one" (Romans 3:10). The fundamental problem with humanity, then, is not a lack of self-esteem. Though poverty and hunger are serious global concerns, they are not the roots of the world's ills. The real problem humans face is *they have no righteousness before God.* Consequently, the wages of sin is death (Romans 6:23)

When we look back at the doctrine of the fall, we are reminded of why this condition exists. Adam and Eve's sin set all of humanity in a state of rebellion against God. It imparted to the human race a sinful nature twisted and turned away from the path of righteousness. Some theologians explain this by calling Adam the "federal head of the human race," while others use the language of "natural headship." Regardless of which position one adopts, we discover in Genesis 3 that humanity's perfect communion and fellowship with God has been broken because of sin. Because mankind thought it could be "like God" (Genesis 3:5) in the Garden, mankind still tries to be its own god—even now.

Exclusive

A further reason why we can call salvation through Christ essential is because the Bible presents Jesus as the only savior. To be exclusive about anything is often unpopular, especially when it comes to religious matters. However, the apostles boldly said the following of Jesus in their diverse religious context: "And there is salvation in no one else, for there is no other name under heaven given among men by which we must be saved" (Acts 4:12). They did not mince their words, nor hold out the hope of salvation through means besides responding to the revelation of God in Christ. As we saw in chapter four, who Jesus is enables Him to do what He does in terms of making salvation possible. But as we will see below, the way the New Testament writers expound upon the life, death, and resurrection of Christ helps to make this connection even more clear.

Sufficient

Because we live in a time where so many religious goods such as conferences, books, and web resources are available, it is easy to look to these to meet our needs. While these tools certainly have their place in pointing us to Christ,

Jesus is sufficient to save sinners and give them the spiritual life they need. The author of Hebrews captures it nicely when he says, "Consequently, he is able to save to the uttermost those who draw near to God through him, since he always lives to make intercession for them" (Hebrews 7:25). This verse is pointing us ahead to two facets of the salvation Christ offers. First, by saying "consequently" and "makes intercession," it leads us to what Christ accomplished. In other words, what are the *grounds* of salvation? Second, by saying "draw near to God," it leads us to the condition of salvation.

The Grounds of Salvation: What Christ Accomplished

Sometimes when Christians speak about being saved, they often don't choose their words carefully. At times, even though we have the best of intentions, we say the reason we're Christians is due to our faith—or perhaps even our obedience. Obviously, this is true in one sense. As we'll see in a moment, faith and repentance are two sides of the same experience of coming to know God in Christ through the Spirit. However, to emphasize that we are saved by our faith apart from further comment is to confuse the condition of salvation with the grounds of salvation. An illustration will perhaps clarify this important point.

Imagine a father instructs his son to clean his room. If he obeys his father's command, this will result in a trip to the zoo. The son hastens to clean his room, carefully attending to every bit of dirt and grime. He vacuums, folds his clothes, and even washes the windows. Upon completion, the father purchases tickets online for the zoo the next day. Now, a simple question to ask the boy is, "Why were you able to go to the zoo?" He will likely answer, "Because I cleaned my room, of course." Most of us would accept this answer and move on. However, the deeper, more fundamental reason for the gift of the zoo trip was not the boy's obedience. Rather, it was the generosity and grace of the father.

While this illustration is a pale comparison to the realities of the Gospel, it helps in some small way to indicate what is happening in conversion. In other words, while faith and repentance are the appropriate responses to God's call to salvation, we must never confuse our role with God's initiative or provision.

Atonement: Propitiation, Mediation, and Substitution

Man's unrighteousness is ultimately what separates him from God. In fact, the Bible warns that the very wrath of God abides on sinners (e.g., John 3:36). Apart from Christ, man stands condemned. What, if anything, can provide acceptance before God? Is there someone who can bridge the gulf fixed between humanity and God? This is where the doctrine of atonement is at the heart of the Good News of Jesus.

Atonement language is found in both the Old and New Testaments. It is related to the sacrificial system God instituted to teach Israel the true cost of sin as well as pointing them to a final, perfect sacrifice that He would eventually provide (e.g., Leviticus 16). These sacrifices were seen as substitutes, yet they could never completely turn God's wrath away from sin. A perfect substitution and sacrifice would be needed if the sin-problem of human beings could be remedied once and for all. Jesus is that remedy.

The Scriptures present Jesus as sinless (e.g., Hebrews 4:15). He, like the lamb of Isaiah 53, is described as one who was spotless and innocent (e.g., 1 Peter 1:19). Therefore, He can be the Savior of lawbreakers because He kept the law perfectly. He satisfies the wrath of God against sin because He actually received the penalty for sins (e.g., 1 Peter 2:24). His death, in other words, was vicarious, or "on behalf of others" (e.g., Mark 10:45; Hebrews 2:9). Furthermore, this is why recognizing Jesus to be fully God and fully man is so important. Only God could satisfy His own holy standard. Likewise, only He could abate His own righteous anger against sin. This is why Jesus' sacrifice was accepted, and yet He was also raised from the dead. His full humanity is an equally important part of His identity. The Old Testament high priest could propitiate for the sins of the people because he was a person, too. Jesus can be a substitute, a sacrifice on their behalf, as well as a great high priest for the human race (e.g., Hebrews 2:14-17).

In all these things, Jesus was turning God's wrath away from sinners (propitiation), inaugurating a new covenant between God and man (mediation), and standing in the place of sinners (substitution). He intercedes on behalf of those incapable of saving themselves. In John Stott's words, "The essence of sin is man substituting himself for God, while the essence of salvation is God substituting himself for man."[1] In these things, we see what the Bible means when it teaches that Jesus purchased us by His own blood from the bondage we once knew (redemption). No wonder the Bible calls these truths "good news"!

The next reasonable question to ask is, "How does one embrace salvation?" The answer is "by grace through faith."

The Condition of Salvation: Faith

Ephesians 2:8 is probably the most-quoted verse when it comes to the conversion of sinners. Paul writes, "For by grace you have been saved through faith. And this is not your own doing; it is the gift of God." How does this happen practically?

By Grace Through Faith

Many Christians were saved during a worship service. Others Christians remember hearing the Gospel presented by a faithful Sunday School teacher and then later expressed their conviction of sin and desire to accept Christ to a parent. Whatever the circumstances of one's conversion, salvation is not only grounded in the work of Jesus Christ, the Holy Spirit also enables it.

One of the important roles of the Holy Spirit is that of convicting. The Scriptures explain this when it says that the Thessalonian Christians accepted Christ because the apostles' message came to them "in the Holy Spirit and with full conviction" (1 Thessalonians 1:5). Near the end of His earthly ministry, Jesus Himself said that the Spirit would come to convict the world of sin, righteousness, and judgment (John 16:8-11). The Holy Spirit, then, is the agent who uses God's Word to convict sinners and draw them to God. Sinners don't come to God on their own terms; they come at the call of God's Spirit who presents the grace of Christ seen in the cross. Faith is not only belief or assent to the facts of the Gospel. After all, even demons are orthodox in their beliefs (e.g., James 2:19). Faith is also trust in Christ for salvation.

Repentance and Regeneration

Some may wonder about the glaring absence of repentance from this explanation. After all, many verses in the New Testament link faith or belief with repentance. First, repentance involves the turning away from sin. It is literally a "change of mind." It means that one is completely turning from one path or direction to head in the opposite direction. Second, "repent and believe" are indeed said to be the conditions of salvation in much of the apostolic preaching and teaching (e.g., Acts 2:37-38; 3:19; 2 Corinthians 7:10). Does this contradict the message of salvation by grace through faith? Not at all. Even in passages that use this language, the authors (many of whom were also the first preachers) no doubt thought repentance to be the unavoidable outcome of true faith. To turn to Christ, looking to Him for deliverance, hope, and life is to also turn *away* from self and all other rival kings. Trusting in Christ requires turning from sin.

When a person is converted, he or she undergoes what the Bible calls regeneration, or "the new birth." It is why many evangelical Christians describe themselves as "born again." They find this language in John 3, where a religious leader named Nicodemus inquires of Christ what it means to know God. Jesus says that one must be born again—namely, "of water and the Spirit" (John 3:5). Some believe this indicates both physical birth as well as spiritual rebirth. However, when considered alongside other biblical passages (e.g., Ezekiel 36), we see that Jesus is probably emphasizing the full, cleansing experience of God's transforming Spirit. Regeneration, then, is a part of conversion.

It is this aspect of conversion where some Christians disagree. Some believe that regeneration *precedes* faith. Faith then is seen as a gift imparted to believers. Others believe faith is actually exercised by individuals *after* God extends a special grace that enables them to respond to His offer of salvation. In other words, faith *precedes* regeneration. There are other elements that accompany these two perspectives, such as what role God's foreknowledge or predetermination plays in the process. Additionally, the doctrine of election is linked biblically with salvation (e.g., Ephesians 1:3-14). What these perspectives have in common is that they both say that God, in some sense, takes the initiative in leading sinners to Himself. They also both insist that faith, repentance, and regeneration are indispensable parts of salvation. From here, a range of opinions will inevitably exist. Yet it is important for Christians to understand the various ways of making sense of the biblical record, while always emphasizing "grace through faith" when it comes to salvation. From there, the gateway to salvation's blessings is opened wide.

The Results of Salvation: Union with Christ

The motif that Protestant Christians have historically used to describe the central blessing of salvation is union with Christ. This phrase makes sense given that without salvation, our fellowship with God is broken. However, when we repent of sin and trust in Christ, we are united with Him in His death as well as His resurrection (e.g., Romans 6:4-6). This signals that we are now reconciled to God. As redemption is a salvific term borrowed from the realm of commerce, reconciliation is a relational or personal term. It isn't merely a new awareness or new way of acting in the world, but it is a "personal encounter from 'outside'."[2] We are restored to right standing with the very God and Father of Jesus who died for us. How is it we stand accepted before a holy and awesome God?

Justification and Adoption

Justification is what happens when guilty sinners are declared innocent by faith in Christ. Once again, our faith is only the *means* of being right with God. The *source* is the grace of God, as seen in the cross. Justification is typically associated with the legal realm—that of the courtroom. The courtroom analogy, of course, isn't perfect. This is because in the biblical scenario, God is the judge before whom we stand, the attorney who pleads our case, and the innocent person who receives the penalty for our crimes. That the righteousness of Christ is credited to our account while He takes upon Himself our sins explains why people in the first century—and even today—are scandalized. This is a salvation we cannot earn.

Adoption is another beautiful part of salvation. It is family-oriented language that describes the privileges imparted to those who come to Christ. God is not only a Sovereign Lord; we also come to know Him as a son would his own father. This Father provides, protects, comforts, and disciplines as a faithful spiritual parent.[3] The practice of legal adoption in many ways embodies the biblical teaching. In effect, a perfect stranger is invited into the home of another to live and enjoy all the benefits of being a biological child of those parents. Remarkably, this is how Romans and Galatians explain spiritual adoption (e.g., Romans 8:12-17; Galatians 4:1-7).

Sanctification

Sanctification is the language the Scriptures use to describe the process by which God sets apart His people for His special purposes. In particular, it refers to purification and cleansing. This is exactly what salvation begins in the Christian life: a process of renewal, restoration, and renovation. God is restoring in us that which was broken in the fall. Some Christians simply describe this as "spiritual growth" or "discipleship." While chapter seven will explore this subject, there are three specific consequences of salvation that make our sanctification possible: (1) Christians are freed from the penalty for sin; (2) Christians are gradually freed from the power of sin; and (3) Christians will eventually be free from the presence of sin. Each of these incredible truths deserves some explanation.

Because Christians are freed from sin's penalty, they experience everlasting life (e.g., John 3:16). Though physical death will still come, death does not have the final say over our existence. Not only are we present with the Lord apart from the body but one day, all believers who have died will be raised, signaling death's final defeat (see chapter twelve) as well as salvation's consequences for the entire creation. But experiencing forgiveness for sins is sufficient to provide peace, even now (e.g., Ephesians 1:7; Colossians 1:14).

Being freed from the power of sin is another result of salvation. Because the Holy Spirit lives in every believer, each has the spiritual strength available to resist temptation and live for God (e.g., 1 Corinthians 10:13; Ephesians 1:13; 4:30b). Christian spirituality is about growing in grace so we walk in the Spirit and not according to our old sinful nature ("the flesh").

Finally, Christians can rejoice and trust in God now because we look to a future day when we will be totally rid of the sin that so easily besets us in this life. This, along with points 1 and 2, reminds us that salvation is presented in Scripture as progressive. This doesn't mean that one cannot be truly saved today. Rather, it means that while our hope is sure in Christ, our journey through life is one in which we are *being saved*, and one day will be *entirely saved* from life in a broken world.

Conclusion

Much more could be said about the glorious truths of the Gospel. Other biblical teachings such as the "sealing of the Holy Spirit" and the curse motif (e.g., Galatians 3:13), offer more insight into the riches of God's grace. However, the Apostle Paul says that for all eternity, Christians will be plumbing the depths of God's salvation (e.g., Ephesians 2:7), so it shouldn't disappoint readers to learn that our study of salvation will conclude here. However, Ephesians 2:10 does say that we are saved "for good works." One of the results of salvation, then, is *preparation*. God's grace prepares us for and motivates us to a particular way of life that involves what the New Testament calls "good works." This is what distinguishes saving faith (living faith) from a faith without works (dead faith). This point will be taken up in the next chapter, where we learn what the Bible teaches about Christian spirituality.

For Further Reading:

Bridges, Jerry. *The Gospel for Real Life*. Colorado Springs, CO: NavPress, 2003. **(B)**

Moore, Russell. *Adopted by God: The Priority of Adoption for Christian Families & Churches*. Wheaton, IL: Crossway, 2009. **(B)**

Picirilli, Robert E. *Grace, Faith, and Free Will: Contrasting Views of Salvation*. Nashville, TN: Randall House, 2002. **(A)**

Stott, John R. W. *The Cross of Christ*. Downers Grove, IL: InterVarsity Press, 1986. **(I)**

---

[1] John R. W. Stott, *The Cross of Christ* (Downers Grove, IL: InterVarsity Press, 1986), 159.

[2] Michael S. Horton, *Covenant and Salvation: Union with Christ* (Louisville, KY: Westminster John Knox Press, 2007), 224.

[3] Jerry Bridges, *The Gospel for Real Life* (Colorado Springs, CO: NavPress, 2003), 132.

7

Spirituality

Surveys conducted around the year 2000 revealed an intriguing trend about the average American's outlook. It showed that while only some of those surveyed considered themselves "religious," a significant majority considered themselves "spiritual."[1] How is it that such a contrast could exist between religion and spirituality? Aren't they related?

There are several probable culprits for this mindset. One reason is that while religion is seen as rigid and inflexible, spirituality is seen as free and open. Claims to absolute truth are unpopular and undesirable because they, by their very nature, exclude those who disagree with us. This is how religious people are often perceived. However, a "spiritual" person can pick and choose beliefs and practices from various worldviews while at the same time be seen as tolerant and permissive. All religious people have is their ancient dogmas or doctrines. Therefore, religion is seen by many as stuffy, confining, and limiting.

A second reason for a dichotomy between spirituality and religion has to do with commitment. Leaders of institutions and organizations in America often decry the lack of commitment among their membership. Studies have shown that civic participation has waned in many communities. Even political parties must work diligently every election cycle just to persuade people to exercise their freedom to vote! This question of commitment, then, encompasses both the desire and willingness to settle on core beliefs, as well as devoting oneself to a community or institution. In the case of Christian sojourners, this institution is the church. Many of the same "spiritual" people consider the church to be a place for religious practitioners but not necessarily a place to find authentic spirituality.

One may wonder why we begin our reflection on spirituality with this analysis. It is helpful because it describes the climate in which many Christians find themselves. It is a climate that resists three essential dimensions of Christian spirituality: doctrine, character, and community.

The Foundation: Grounded in the Gospel

When Christians talk about "spirituality," they are usually referring to the biblical doctrine of *sanctification*. As we saw in chapter six, sanctification is the work that God initiates upon conversion. He has freed us from the penalty for sin. He gradually frees us from sin's power. And when He returns, He will deliver us from the complete presence of sin. But what does spirituality look like in the present?

Rooted in Christ

There is no true spirituality apart from Christ. Without God as its reference point, spirituality floats around like a ship without a rudder. This is the message that echoes throughout the pages of the New Testament, which emphasizes a very important relationship—the one between justification and sanctification. Justification is a once-and-for-all declaration. It is what happens when God renders an innocent verdict concerning sinners. This is only for those covered in Christ's righteousness by faith. It is objective and definitive. Yet at this same moment, sanctification begins in the Christian life. While it is progressive, it also signals an immediate change in the human heart and the promise of eternal life. A new nature is imparted to the Christian. Christians are now able to begin the journey toward Christlikeness that we sometimes call discipleship or spiritual growth. Broadly, it is called spirituality.

Some will be surprised to find that despite the immediate blessings that accompany salvation, God is not content to leave us where we are. He is, in fact, taking us somewhere—deeper and deeper into the knowledge of the Lord Jesus Christ. As we grow in grace, our lives inevitably change. But this transformation is gradual. We might say that "growth in God's grace is a process and not an event."[2] As we consider the grounds of Christian spirituality, it is also important we consider the agent who brings it about. To be sure, when a person becomes a Christian, he experiences each member of the Trinity. As Francis Schaeffer says, we relate to God the Father as adopted children, we enjoy union with Christ our Savior, and we are indwelt by the Holy Spirit.[3] It is the Holy Spirit who is especially important to consider because the Bible typically highlights His role in sanctification. The Holy Spirit's work was described partly in chapter five, but here some additional reflection is necessary.

Led by the Spirit

The late biblical scholar F. F. Bruce surmises the Holy Spirit's role well. He notes that scripturally, especially in Paul's letters, "it is the province of the Holy Spirit within the people of Christ to reproduce his likeness increasingly in their lives, but the consummation of this sanctifying work awaits the day of Christ."[4] The Spirit works in us to continually point to the person of Christ. This is why sometimes the "Spirit of Christ" is a phrase used in the Bible that is synonymous with Holy Spirit (e.g., Philippians 1:19). Jesus' disciples especially came to recognize this in the earliest days of their ministry, when His message from John 14–17 came to fruition. The Helper that Jesus spoke of came and reminded them of all He had taught them (e.g., John 14:26; 16:13). He empowered them for ministry (Acts 1:5; 4:8). He even gave gifts to the church (and still does today!). While some traditions differ in emphasis about the Holy Spirit's work, Scripture clearly teaches that He comforts, empowers, convicts, and grants personal transformation.

Set Apart and Pursuing Holiness

To sanctify something means to set it apart or make it holy. In the Old Testament it is linked to the ceremonial cleanness of the items used and participants in the worship of God. Israel's God repeatedly said to her: "You shall therefore be holy, for I am holy" (e.g., Leviticus 11:45). Holiness, according to J. I. Packer, "means being near God, like God, given to God, and pleasing God."[5] He expands on this by saying that true holiness is "God-taught, Spirit-wrought Christ-likeness, the sum and substance of committed discipleship, the demonstration of faith working by love, the responsive outflow in righteousness of supernatural life from the hearts of those who are born again."[6] God's holy ones, then, are set apart for His special purposes in the world.

It is important we discern the link between identity and conduct. Biblically, there is a particular way of life consistent with being a child of God. Notice the way the following passage links our identity as God's people with our behavior in the world:

> But you are a chosen race, a royal priesthood, a holy nation, a people for his own possession, that you may proclaim the excellencies of him who called you out of darkness into his marvelous light. Once you were not a people, but now you are God's people; once you had not received mercy, but now you have received mercy. Beloved, I urge you as sojourners and exiles to abstain from the passions of the flesh, which wage war against your soul. Keep your conduct among the Gentiles honorable, so that when they speak against you as evildoers, they may see your good deeds and glorify God on the day of visitation.

(1 Peter 2:9-12)

Peter borrows the Old Testament's language about Israel and applies it to Christians (e.g., Exodus 19:5-6a; Deuteronomy 7:6). It is this distinct identity that is the grounds for their holy testimony in the world. As we will see in the next chapter, this is where our understanding of the church must be forged. Christians are in the world, but are not characterized by its desires, priorities, and commitments (e.g., John 17). Their holiness sets them apart. Yet all true holiness begins with Jesus Christ. While this is a doctrinal point, it also emphasizes the character, to which our contemporary society is so averse. However, it is the very thing designed to impact them for Christ.

Restoration and Renovation

Our sanctification can also be envisioned by the twin images of restoration and renovation. The Bible teaches that Christ is the image of God (e.g., 2 Corinthians 4:4; Colossians 1:15). All of the fullness of God bodily dwells in Him. So when we think about our sanctification, this literally means God is, through His Spirit, conforming us to the image of Christ (Romans 8:29). Ephesians 4:24 calls us to embrace our new selves. This new nature is "created after the likeness of God in true righteousness and holiness." Colossians 3:10 picks up this same thread of "out with the old and in with the new," to use our modern-day jargon. Paul says we have put off the old self (pre-conversion) and should embrace the new self (salvation life) "which is being renewed in knowledge after the image of its creator." This is a picture of restoration.

However, this change also involves the renovation and renewal of character. A biblical metaphor is that of a potter molding clay into a particular shape. God is the potter, and His followers are the clay who allow Him to mold them as He wishes. Our willingness to receive such transformation might be captured by the word *obedience*. We have certainly been set free from the law's ability to only show us our sin. Christ, after all, has kept the law where we could not. Yet God's commandments should become our delight as Christians. In fact, our obedience shows our true loyalty: "If you love me, you will keep my commandments" (John 14:15). John quotes Jesus here, but likely has in mind the two great commandments that encapsulate the rest: Love God supremely, and your neighbor as yourself (e.g., Matthew 22:34-40).

The Apostle John continues this theme of obedience in his first epistle, where he echoes that our assurance of salvation (which is part of Christian spirituality) is grounded in a present walk with the Lord. True spirituality, then, is not just about mystical experiences or encounters with the divine. It is about the daily renovation God is doing in the heart—a project He began at the moment of our new birth. We often talk about "growing pains" as kids move from one stage of growth to another. The same imagery can be applied to Christian maturity. It is seldom easy though always essential. The cross of Christ and the indwelling of the Spirit are indeed the grounds of sanctification. However, because spirituality is a process that includes many dimensions of life, we must ask what are the *means* of such a transformation. How does maturity happen?

The Means: His Word

Once we understand that our heavenly Father's plan for His children is grounded in the work of Christ and carried out by the Holy Spirit, we will naturally ask, "How does He do this?" Quite simply, the Spirit and Word are God's appointed means to make us like Jesus. The Spirit uses the inspired Word of God to instruct, convict, comfort, and persuade Christians to the path of righteousness. Consider the following passages:

> Your word is a lamp to my feet and a light to my path.
> (Psalm 119:105)

> For the word of God is living and active, sharper than any two-edged sword, piercing to the division of soul and of spirit, of joints and of marrow, and discerning the thoughts and intentions of the heart.
> (Hebrews 4:12)

While justification (Christ's definitive work) is the grounds for our walk with the Lord, the Word (as used by the Spirit) is the means that paves the pathway for this walk. God, in the New Testament, pours His Spirit within the hearts of His people, and His written word becomes a means for giving them direction concerning His will. Notice the way Peter makes this connection:

> His divine power has granted to us all things that pertain to life and godliness, through the knowledge of him who called us to his own glory and excellence, by which he has granted to us his precious and very great promises, so that through them you may become partakers of the divine nature, having escaped from the corruption that is in the world because of sinful desire.
> (2 Peter 1:3-4)

As this passage indicates, God's power (which is often linked with the Holy Spirit) and God's Word (described by the language of "promises") enable us to live holy lives. What obstacles, then, does this powerful Word enable us to overcome?

Resistance and Refinement: Discipleship

Galatians 5:17 warns that the desires of our old, fleshly self and those of our new, Spirit-led self are constantly at war. This only amplifies the seriousness of temptation. This is why Jesus' temptations from earlier are so helpful. They show

He is able to sympathize with us in our trials (Hebrews 2:18). Jesus shows that God is always faithful to grant an escape route from temptation (1 Corinthians 10:13). However, our old desires and external temptations aren't the only challenges we face. As previously stated, growth happens in the crucible of everyday life. This refinement involves countless hardships, such as persecution and physical suffering. Yet there are some important, biblical practices that utilize God's appointed means—His Spirit using His *Word*—to help us walk with Him daily. We call these *spiritual disciplines*.

Once our identity and hope as Christians has been grounded in Jesus Christ, we want to pursue holiness full throttle. But discipleship isn't easy. Following a crucified Jewish carpenter in the first century was no easier than following Him today. Just consider two other forms of the word discipleship: disciple and discipline. We know from the ministry of Jesus that being His disciple didn't result in great popularity. And certainly discipline is often an unpleasant experience. However, both being a disciple and being disciplined demonstrate our authenticity as followers and children of God. The author of Hebrews even reminds us "the Lord disciplines the one he loves, and chastises every son whom he receives" (Hebrews 12:6). The good news is that in the midst of being a disciple or a child of the living God, there are some basic tools that can help us press forward. Let's consider these tools for the task.

Bible Study

Bible study is indispensable to the Christian life. We find, especially in the so-called pastoral epistles (1–2 Timothy and Titus) admonitions to study the Word in order to be equipped for life and ministry (e.g., 2 Timothy 2:15). It would be easy for this habit to be relegated to preachers and teachers alone. Yet evangelical Christians believe in the priesthood of all believers. This means that all believers have equal access to God by virtue of Christ's priesthood for them. Therefore, while we may have leaders in churches, they are not the gatekeepers to spiritual growth. In fact, it is essential that lay Christians study the Word if they are to obey God in the day-to-day rhythm of life.

Prayer

Prayer is another spiritual discipline that has been sometimes called our "lifeline to God." It comes in the form of thanksgiving and praise, petitions, and even lamentation. One might wonder what this has to do with utilizing God's Word. However, we find countless prayers included in the Scriptures that offer some guidance on what ought to be a priority in the way we pray. Our prayer life is said to be aided by Spirit (e.g., Romans 8:26-27; Jude 20b). Prayer is indeed a spiritual discipline because it allows the Word to shape our expectations and the Spirit to guide our utterances.

Fasting

Fasting is a lost art for many American Christians. The word itself conjures up images of monks withdrawn from society, praying hours on end and fasting in their secluded monasteries. Our modern dieting programs also hinder us from understanding the *spiritual* dimensions of refraining from eating. Some will even question whether this practice has a place in Christian spirituality. Jesus clearly answers this doubt in Matthew 6:16-18. He does not begin His remarks by saying, "If you fast." Rather, He begins by saying, "When you fast." Scripture assumes, then, that believers would occasionally fast; it is a reflection of our longing for God's kingdom to come. It also demonstrates our total dependence on God as the bread of life as opposed to the daily bread that too often becomes primary.

Worship

Romans 12:1-2 says that our bodies should be offered as living sacrifices to God, which becomes an act of worship unto God. These verses capture the larger notion of worship in Scripture, which sees all of life as worship unto God. This is also seen in John 4, when Jesus says true worshippers should worship in Spirit and in truth. He is speaking about the heart of the worshiper (regenerated) and to the mind of the worshiper (rightly fixed on Christ). One can quickly discern how spirituality and worship could, in a sense, be seen as two sides of the same coin. Our morality or maturity as Christians is very much a part of our worship (e.g., Psalms 15; 17).

However, there is also a narrow sense to worship. This involves the weekly gathering that we do with other Christians. While much of our worship discussion will be reserved for chapter nine, the *communal aspect* of Christian spirituality must not be overlooked. The community of Christians—the church—is the main area where the outcome of Christian spirituality is visible. It is what we might call God's "disciple-forming institution." The worship of the church arises out of this institution's environment, where good works and spiritual fruit are tangible, authentic, and overflowing.

The Outcome: Good Works and Spiritual Fruit

Ephesians 2 has been considered already because it is crucial for understanding both salvation and spirituality. The passage concludes with verse 10, which is central to Christian spirituality: "For we are his workmanship, created in Christ Jesus for good works, which God prepared beforehand, that we should walk in them." Salvation by grace opens us to our God-given purpose in life, which is to be rich in good works. We could describe these works in terms of sacrifice, obedience, and even mission. But they are also acts of grace and love produced in the lives of Christians because of the Spirit's work.

Titus steers us clear of any confusion about whether God's grace or our works come first: God saved us "not because of works done by us in righteousness," and yet the salvation by grace paves the way for us to "devote [ourselves] to good works" (Titus 3:5, 8). However, where do these good works show up? They are revealed *in community*. This is why so many modern understandings of spirituality fail—because they are individualistic, not communal. They leave out the loving expressions of kindness to *others*. Our good works are performed unto *others*, especially those in the household of faith (Galatians 6:10).

This same pattern is true of spiritual fruit. Paul, in Galatians 5:16-25, contrasts two options: We can either follow the desires of our flesh, which will result in all sorts of rotten fruit (bad works). Or we can walk in the Spirit, which will, in turn, produce good fruit. While these fruits are described using language we often associate with virtue (love, joy, peace, patience, etc.), this fruit is only evident *in relationship to others*. So when Christians are growing in the Lord, they are rich in good works and they produce spiritual fruit. The Bible also teaches that such Christians are using their spiritual gifts. Spiritual gifts are special endowments to Christians in the church, given by the Holy Spirit for the service of God's people. More will be said about these in chapter nine, but this is another place where the Holy Spirit is relevant to Christian spirituality and spirituality to the church.

Conclusion

Growth is not just an idea worth striving for; it is what Christians are called to (e.g., Ephesians 4:14-16; Hebrews 6:1; 1 Peter 2:2). Christians are, after all, God's "new creation" (2 Corinthians 5:17). This new creation certainly differs from what we might expect. Christians are called to be slaves to a new master (Romans 6:15-19). They are called to die to self (Romans 14:8). They are warned about rushing to the front of the line in life (Matthew 20:16, 25-27). They are even called to embrace weakness, for in it they find strength (2 Corinthians 12:9-10). These paradoxes baffle the unbeliever, but for the one following Christ, they gradually make sense.

Christian spirituality requires both doctrine and discipleship. Our beliefs and convictions must be grounded in sound thinking about God. But there must also be practices or habits in which we are fostered. Yet God wants this to be a wholehearted, authentic effort. So our discipleship even includes our desires. Being like Jesus involves all of our being—what Leroy Forlines calls our "total personality."[7] This process of formation happens in a community called the church. We might say that there are internal factors that nourish our growth (doctrine) and external factors that provide the right environment for growth (disciplines and community). His grace is the soil out of which our lives bloom and as they bloom, they produce fruit as would a healthy tree.

Becoming an honorable vessel useful to God is hardly a short, simple process (2 Timothy 2:20-21). It takes grace-energized effort. It requires a Spirit-led, Word-saturated life. The book of Titus, however, summarizes it best:

> For the grace of God has appeared, bringing salvation for all people, training us to renounce ungodliness and worldly passions, and to live self-controlled, upright, and godly lives in the present age, waiting for our blessed hope, the appearing of the glory of our great God and Savior Jesus Christ, who gave himself for us to redeem us from all lawlessness and to purify for himself a people for his own possession who are zealous for good works.

(Titus 2:11-14)

God's grace is not only enough to save us, but also enough to sanctify. It is the *community* in which this sanctification transpires that will be the subject of chapters eight and nine.

For Further Reading:

Bonhoeffer, Dietrich. *The Cost of Discipleship.* New York: Touchstone, 1995. **(A)**

Bridges, Jerry. *The Pursuit of Holiness.* Colorado Springs, CO: NavPress, 1978. **(B)**

Lane, Timothy, and Paul Tripp. *How People Change.* Greensboro, NC: New Growth Press, 2008. **(B)**

Ryle, J. C. *Holiness: Its Nature, Hindrances, Difficulties, and Roots.* Peabody, MA: Hendrickson Publishers, 2007. **(I)**

Schaeffer, Francis. *True Spirituality.* Carol Stream, IL: Tyndale House Publishers, 2001. **(I)**

---

[1] David F. Wells, *Above All Earthly Pow'rs: Christ in a Postmodern World* (Grand Rapids, MI: Eerdmans, 2005), 110-114.

[2] Tim Lane and Paul Tripp, *How People Change* (Greensboro, NC: New Growth Press, 2008), 36.

[3] Francis Schaeffer, *True Spirituality* (Carol Stream, IL: Tyndale House Publishers, 2001), 67-68.

[4] F. F. Bruce, *The Epistle to the Colossians, to Philemon, and to the Ephesians* (NICNT) (Grand Rapids, MI: Eerdmans, 1984), 137.

[5] J. I. Packer, *Keep in Step with the Spirit* (Old Tappan, NJ: Revell, 1984), 95.

[6] Ibid, 97.

[7] F. Leroy Forlines, *The Quest for Truth: Answering Life's Inescapable Questions* (Nashville, TN: Randall House, 2001), 225.

8

The Church: Origin and Identity

What is the church? Where did it come from? Whose idea was it? Christians sometimes ask these questions as well as those who pass our places of worship. Some probably assume the church was a creation of religious zealots many centuries ago. Others will perhaps see the church as a glorified moralist club with nothing better to do than condemn the decisions of others. Still others who may have received financial aid in the past from a local church or even attended a Vacation Bible School program as children will have a positive outlook. Regardless of the perceptions, Christians must be prepared to give a reason for the hope within (1 Peter 3:15). This inevitably will include an account for how our hope takes shape among Christians. These other Christians are a part of a community—a community called the church.

In this chapter, we will consider the church's origin and identity. This will include some reflection on God's people throughout Scripture, including the church's foundation. We will also consider some of the metaphors the New Testament uses to describe the church.

A People for His Name

The God of a nation is shown in that nation's character. We could also say that the character of a nation is shaped by its God. In the ancient world, this was no doubt the case for Israel among other nations. The design of God was for them to be holy as He was holy. In turn, the nations would see that Israel's God was real. He was the Lord God, the self-existent One who is Lord over all nations. However, even prior to Israel's birth as a people, God had a *people*.

In the beginning, Adam and Eve were God's people. They enjoyed a special relationship with their Creator. Yet through the deceitfulness of pride, their sin spoiled that relationship. Wickedness breaks forth at every turn when Cain commits the first murder (Genesis 4:8), Lamech becomes the first polygamist (Genesis 4:19), and wickedness pervades the earth (Genesis 6:5). God still demonstrates His relentless love by preserving a people—Noah's family—even in the face of a global flood (Genesis 7-9). But shameful behavior and rebellion continue beyond the judgment of the floodwaters (Genesis 10-11).

Genesis 12:1-3, however, removes any doubt about God's interest in people. He graciously chooses Abram and promises to make a great nation out of this elderly nobody and his barren wife (e.g., Genesis 17). Through a remarkable set of circumstances, God indeed raises up a nation through Abram (later Abraham). Unfortunately, it seems like God's plans are short-circuited by 430 years of servitude in Egypt! Yet the Scriptures remind us that the cries of the people came up to God and He heard their groans (Exodus 2:23-25). God then brings the Hebrews out of Egypt in spectacular fashion. Yet this deliverance comes with conditions: They must keep the covenant He makes with them at Sinai (Exodus 20) if He will bless Israel over and against the nations. Exodus 19 demonstrates this:

> Now therefore, if you will indeed obey my voice and keep my covenant, you shall be my treasured possession among all peoples, for all the earth is mine; and you shall be to me a kingdom of priests and a holy nation.

> (Exodus 19:5-6a)

These were not only Moses' marching orders to communicate to the people; this is a promise that through obedience Israel's identity would be secured, and thus Israel would be able to fulfill God's mission for them in the world. Unfortunately, throughout the Old Testament we see their constant failure to hear and obey God's law. This is why God raises up the prophets to call Israel to corporate repentance. Their identity as God's people is questionable, given their wickedness. In the midst of the woes and disturbing images emanating from the prophets' lips, a word of hope breaks forth:

> Behold, the days are coming, declares the LORD, when I will make a new covenant with the house of Israel and the house of Judah, not like the covenant that I made with their fathers on the day when I took them by the hand to bring them out of the land of Egypt, my covenant that they broke, though I was their husband, declares the LORD For this is the covenant that I will make with the house of Israel after those days, declares the LORD: I will put my law within them, and I will write it on their hearts. And I

will be their God, and they shall be my people. And no longer shall each one teach his neighbor and each his brother, saying, "Know the LORD," for they shall all know me, from the least of them to the greatest, declares the LORD. For I will forgive their iniquity, and I will remember their sin no more.

(Jeremiah 31:31-34)

God is preparing to do something new among His people. A new covenant will be made and inaugurated by His Messiah.

The New Covenant: Message and People

When Jesus celebrated the Passover with His disciples, He said that the cup, representing His shed blood, began a new covenant (e.g., Luke 22:20; 1 Corinthians 11:25). Christ mediates a better covenant with better promises (e.g., 2 Corinthians 3:7-11; Hebrews 8:6-13; 12:24). So who is included in this covenant? New Testament Christians, just like the Old Testament Israelites, are people said to be His chosen people—a kingdom of priests (1 Peter 2:9a). The new covenant involves salvation in Christ and becoming subjects in His kingdom (see chapter twelve). It includes the promise of eternal life through faith in the Gospel of Christ. This promise, we might say, is itself the message. Jesus is Savior and Lord and therefore must be recognized as the king over all (e.g., Philippians 2:8-11). But a covenant also involves a people. For the old covenant, it was primarily Israel. What about the new covenant?

The beauty of the new covenant is that all are welcome through Christ by faith. The former boundaries that divided Jew from Gentile are no longer intact (e.g. Ephesians 2:11-22). But can both groups fit under the same roof? According to Jesus, absolutely. In Matthew 16:13-20, Jesus asks His disciples a crucial question: "Who do people say that the Son of Man is?" They offer several possibilities. However, Jesus wants to know who *they* think He is. Peter offers the right answer: "You are the Christ, the Son of the living God." It isn't enough, though, that Peter is correct. Jesus must help the disciples understand the big picture of their confession:

> And I tell you, you are Peter, and on this **rock** I will build my **church**, and the gates of hell shall not prevail against it. I will give you the **keys of the kingdom** of heaven, and whatever you bind on earth shall be bound in heaven, and whatever you loose on earth shall be loosed in heaven.

(Matthew 16:18-19, emphasis added)

"Church"

The word translated as "church" in our English Bibles comes from a Greek word *ekklesia* (the study of the church is known as "ecclesiology"). *Ekklesia* most literally means "called-out ones." A more useful, tangible term for what it means is "assembly." This means that most of the time in the New Testament, the word "church" refers to local assemblies of believers (local churches). In some cases, such as Matthew 16, it refers to Christ establishing a visible institution of believers. More will be said on this distinction at the conclusion of this chapter.

"This Rock"

Catholicism has traditionally taught Peter as the rock, thinking him to be the first pope. The context and grammar, however, suggests that we are better positioned to think that Peter's fallible life is hardly capable of being the foundation of Christ's church. Jesus had in mind something more durable: the apostolic *message*. Of course, this includes people! As the church father Tertullian once said, "The blood of the martyrs is the seed of the church." Because the church is a people, we shouldn't be dismissive of the human role in this grand construction project. However, it is the confession that "Christ is Lord" that is the true foundation of the church. This is why, as we will see later, we can affirm the legitimacy of other churches in the world, while differing on doctrinal matters that distinguish us in this life.

"Keys to the Kingdom"

Entering God's kingdom means coming under the rule of Christ by faith (e.g., Matthew 5:20; 7:21). The "keys to the kingdom" is not authorizing the church to do whatever it wants; it stands under Christ's authority. It also isn't a sign that the church is infallible. However, it does mean that Christ is establishing a spiritual institution on earth, guided by heaven's priorities. This means they are accountable to the Lord, and their decisions about membership, discipline, and ministry must be guided by the Word. The church then, as Jonathan Leeman puts it, "is a group of Christians who regularly gather in Christ's name to officially affirm and oversee one another's membership in Jesus Christ and his kingdom through gospel preaching and gospel ordinances."[1]

More explanation will be given in the next chapter about how the church's identity informs its mission and ministry. However, we will now consider some of the images the New Testament presents concerning the church.

Snapshots of the Church

Family of God

In many churches the labels "brother" and "sister" enjoy widespread usage. We know that words like "reverend" are religious jargon, but the language associated with family is more consistent with the church's identity. Jesus publicly declared, "Whoever does the will of my Father in heaven is my brother and sister and mother" (Matthew 12:50; Mark 3:35). Even after the disciples had abandoned Him, on the dawn of His resurrection, He referred to them as "brothers." (e.g., John 20:17). The apostles will constantly use the language of brother and sister to not only begin and end their epistles, but also to supply the substance.

The word "children" also takes on new meaning because we are like spiritual children living under our Father's roof. As we saw in chapter six, adoption is at the heart of salvation. Being adopted, then, also fits with the metaphor of the family. This metaphor is connected with a third: the bride of Christ.

Bride of Christ

In the same way that marriage is the most fundamental relationship in society, it is fundamental to illustrating a spiritual union—that between Christ and His church. The church is said to be His bride, and the Scriptures teach that Jesus is the "bridegroom" (or more simply, the "groom"). Ephesians 5 is the most well-known place where this metaphor is used. Paul calls the submission of a wife and the husband's love to mirror the relationship between Christ and His church. The wife's submission is to her husband's leadership. Yet the husband is charged with a higher degree of love—it is one of ultimate sacrifice that attends to his wife with such care, affection, and self-forgetfulness. This, Paul says, is exactly what Christ has done for His body—His bride, the church.

Another way this marital union is exemplified is when the Gospel writers connect it to Christ's second coming. Jesus told several parables to show how the emotional vitality between a groom and his bride is emblematic of a spiritual vitality between Christ and His church. In Matthew 9, Jesus teaches that fasting is meaningful as a demonstration of expectation and longing *only in the absence* of the groom. He wanted His disciples to see that their fasting should be delayed while He was with them, and practiced only in anticipation of His second coming when the marriage supper of the Lamb would be the wedding feast to end all feasts (Revelation 19:6-8). Later in Matthew 25, Jesus extends the metaphor to include virgins having their lamps adequately prepared to watch for the coming of the bridegroom.

Metaphors, by their very nature, represent a true relationship that exists between two things, yet they are also limited representations. In the same way, the marriage that exists between Christ and the church is an imperfect marriage. It isn't that the husband is unfaithful, but that the bride is. As mentioned above, this relates especially to the Old Testament where Israel is often called an unfaithful bride, guilty of a form of idolatry called *adultery* (e.g., Jeremiah 3:9; 5:7). Yet our relationship as members of the church with our husband the Lord is incomplete also because our relationship hasn't been consummated. As a husband and wife should wait to express the most intimate form of union on the night of their wedding, our ideal union with God will not be enjoyed until the second coming of Christ.

Body of Christ

Although more will be said concerning this metaphor in chapter nine, it is important here to note its prevalence in the New Testament. On the one hand, it is used to emphasize the church's unity. What better way could the Apostle Paul communicate the oneness and diversity of the church? After all, we have all been united because of Christ's sacrificial death (e.g., Ephesians 2:11-22). Yet we are distinct individuals with our own spiritual gifts and biographies (e.g., 1 Corinthians 12–14). There is no better earthly picture of such a phenomenon than the human body. On the other hand, it is also used to express the idea of authority. Christ is said to be head of the church (e.g., Colossians 1:18). In some passages, this conveys that He is the source of the church's life, while in others it emphasizes His lordship over His people. In the same way one's head is central to the healthy operation of one's body, so a church apart from Christ is no church at all![2]

Temple of the Holy Spirit

The ancient world was well acquainted with temples. Temples checkered the Roman Empire as fast-food establishments now fill the intersections of American suburbs. However, Jesus' perspective on temples as sacred sites differed slightly from those in the first century. In perhaps His most controversial remarks, Jesus quipped to some temple-gazers, "Destroy this temple, and in three days I will raise it up" (John 2:19). They were scandalized because they were thinking of a physical object to be venerated; Jesus was thinking of Himself. His crucified and risen body would function as a temple that was the true entry point to God's presence. This is reminiscent of Hebrews 10:19-22 (emphasis added):

> Therefore, brothers, since we have confidence to enter the *holy
> places* by the blood of Jesus, by the new and living way that he
> opened for us *through the curtain*, that is, through his flesh, and
> since we have a great priest over the *house of God*, let us draw
> near with a true heart in full assurance of faith, with our hearts

sprinkled clean from an evil conscience and our bodies washed
with pure water.

The connection between Old Covenant worship, the priesthood of Jesus, and
the spiritual transformation possible through Christ is obvious in this passage.

The indwelling of the Holy Spirit, as we saw in chapter seven, is one of the
blessings of salvation. Yet what this effectively does is transform all of life. All of
our steps, overseen by God, become a part of what it means to be a living sacrifice
(e.g., Romans 12:1-2). Jesus has taken our place on the altar of sacrifice, and now
we are freed to live changed lives. A metaphor that helps us understand what
this means is the temple of the Holy Spirit.

In the midst of warnings against sexual immorality, pagan worship, and faithful stewardship, Paul says to the Corinthian Christians: Your body is a temple
of the Holy Spirit (1 Corinthians 3:16-17; 6:19). In one instance, he also says that
Christians are God's building (1 Corinthians 3:9b). Often these verses are used to
emphasize stewardship of one's physical body. In other words, this verse is interpreted *individualistically*. However, this passage is primarily intended to communicate that the *church* constitutes God's new Spirit-filled temple. First, the
references in 1 Corinthians are emphatically plural ("you" = "you all"). Second,
this same imagery is used by other apostles such as Peter, who calls Christians
"living stones" who offer "spiritual sacrifices," with Christ being the cornerstone
of God's *new* house (1 Peter 2:4-5). This temple is not a building; it is a people.

One, Yet Many?

One final issue that often causes confusion among evangelicals is the very
language of "church." Scripture teaches that there are two churches: a universal, invisible church, and a visible, local church. The first is what the Apostles'
Creed means when it refers to the "Holy Catholic Church" with "Catholic" simply meaning *universal*. Another helpful way of explaining this principle is to
distinguish between "Church" and "the church." "Capital C" Church refers to
all Christians at all times and in all places. When Christians gather in their
Midwestern suburb on Sunday morning, they can rejoice knowing that they are
part of a larger Church assembling to worship the same God in the same Spirit
that day. This is the universal Church.

At the same time, we belong to local churches ("lowercase c")—whether they
be Baptist, Presbyterian, Methodist, or otherwise. These constitute legitimate
churches guided by certain convictions about how they are to organize themselves to practice the faith. Naturally, if these are churches of an evangelical
stripe, they will be committed to the Gospel. They are founded on the words of
Peter: "You are the Christ, the Son of the living God." If Jesus is the Christ (Mes-

siah), then He brings salvation (e.g., Isaiah 61). If He is the Son of the living God, co-equal with God, then all churchly authority derives from Him. This means that in all things, we seek to honor His words (Scripture). Therefore, Protestant evangelical churches, for all their diversity, have much in common.

Conclusion

One doesn't have to be a Christian to understand the value of identity and community. Psychologists, sociologists, and experts in other disciplines frequently study and argue for their legitimacy. Knowing who we are and belonging to others in healthy relationships are key ingredients to a life that flourishes. As we saw in chapter seven, Christian spirituality requires a certain kind of nourishment and environment if it is to bloom. Here we have seen what that environment is; it is a kind of spiritual habitat initiated by God, rooted in Christ, and sustained by the Holy Spirit. Yet it is perhaps difficult to see how the identity of the church translates into the *practices* of the church. While the previously mentioned metaphors serve as a foundation for thinking about the church's purpose and other characteristics, they are just the beginning. In chapter nine, we will explore the mission and ministry of the church.

For Further Reading:

Clowney, Edmund. *The Church (Contours of Christian Theology)*. Downers Grove, IL: IVP Academic, 1995. **(A)**

Dever, Mark. *The Church: The Gospel Made Visible*. Nashville, TN: B&H Academic, 2012. **(I)**

Schaeffer, Francis. *The Church Before the Watching World: A Practical Ecclesiology*. Downers Grove, IL: InterVarsity Press, 1971. **(B)**

---

[1] Jonathan Leeman, *Church Membership: How the World Knows Who Represents Jesus* (Wheaton, IL: Crossway, 2012), 52.

[2] I am indebted to John S. Hammett's book *Biblical Foundations for Baptist Churches: A Contemporary Ecclesiology* (Grand Rapids, MI: Kregel, 2005) for his discussion of this metaphor.

9

The Church: Mission and Ministry

One of the reasons why employees sometimes encounter difficulties on the job is because they don't understand what their employer expects of them. The employee may be a skilled, competent, trustworthy person—even his or her salary may demonstrate that they are a valuable part of the team. However, understanding who the person is and what he is capable of isn't enough to make him a good employee. He needs to receive a job description that outlines: (1) what tasks, responsibilities, and goals he is responsible for, and (2) what tools are at his disposal to accomplish these. Identity and mission go hand-in-hand.

This everyday analogy relates directly to the second half of our study of the church. Recognizing the church as God's idea is the starting point for thinking properly about the church. Otherwise, we might emphasize our authority and our power as opposed to Christ's authority and the Spirit's power! Now that we understand the church is founded on the Gospel and is led by the Spirit, we must consider the mission and ministry of the church. What specifically is the church here on earth to do? How will we fulfill that mission? What constitutes a healthy, evangelical church? These are the questions we will seek to answer.

The Nature of the Mission

Every word of Jesus recorded in Scripture should be considered precious to Christians. But among Jesus' final words to His disciples are these:

> And Jesus came and said to them, "All authority in heaven and on earth has been given to me. Go therefore and make disciples of all nations, baptizing them in the name of the Father and of the

Son and of the Holy Spirit, teaching them to observe all that I have commanded you. And behold, I am with you always, to the end of the age."

(Matthew 28:18-20)

This passage is commonly referred to as the Great Commission. It has been the banner waved over countless mission agencies, evangelistic campaigns, and sermons on sharing the Gospel with others. Most importantly, this is the command issued to the earliest disciples who witnessed the birth of the church (the day of Pentecost) and the growth of the early church. Therefore, this passage deserves our close attention.

"Authority"

Christ's resurrection confirmed something very important about His identity: He was God's anointed king. He had come to establish His kingdom "on earth as it is in heaven" (Matthew 6:10). He has kingdom authority. Therefore, He is able to issue marching orders to the citizens who live under His rule. This does not mean that the church does not exist as people in this world—citizens of various nations. However, it does mean our ultimate loyalty is to King Jesus. We minister in *His name*. Our perspective on earthly authority in the world and the church derives from His Word.

"Go...All Nations"

When we survey the Scriptures, we find through example that the call to missionary efforts abroad isn't for everyone. All Christians are "called" in one sense: They have heard the call of God to salvation and responded in faith and repentance. However, not all are literally called to go to a foreign country. This phrase literally reads something akin to "as you are going." In the context of Christian life—whether it is in a suburb, a slum, or a nomadic tribe—we are to share this Good News about Christ. Some Christians will only live and witness in "Jerusalem and Judea," while others may go to "Samaria and the uttermost parts" (Acts 1:8). The mission of the church is local and global.

"Make Disciples"

What is especially peculiar about the aforementioned passage is that it does not say to make conversions or professions of faith. Of course, these will occur, but Christ does not make the tidy distinction between "convert" and "disciple" that we often make. They are assumed to be part of the true aim of the Gospel: to recognize Christ as Savior and Lord with all of its consequences for our life. A disciple is basically a follower or a learner, yet as we see from Jesus' ministry with His disciples, it involves both the right profession ("You are the Christ") and the right path ("Take up your cross and follow me"). Sacrificial life follows salvation in the biblical outlook.

It is worth noting that we see a shift occur from the Gospels to Acts in what Jesus' followers are called. They are mainly called disciples (followers or learners) in the Gospels, but apostles (sent ones) in Acts. While the term "apostle" is reserved for those commissioned by Jesus, it does enhance our perspective of what it means to follow and obey. History tells us that most of the apostles died as martyrs; they were killed for their testimony to the truth. They obviously didn't arrive overnight in their commitment; spiritual maturity or discipleship takes time. But the Great Commission is about authentic salvation that produces mature disciples.

"Baptizing"

One may not expect a discussion of ordinances (sacraments, for some) to be a part of Christ's plans for the church. Weren't all the old covenant rituals done away with because of the cross? Actually, the new covenant church (like every community) has its important symbols. These aren't just sentimental in nature. They, in fact, teach timeless truths and display spiritual commitments. Baptism has been the most important Christian rite throughout the centuries. It signals entry into the community of faith. Nearly all evangelical churches require baptism for official membership, so they essentially agree on its necessity. What separate some evangelicals—for example, Baptists from Presbyterians—are the meaning, mode, and subjects of baptism.

For many, the basic meaning of baptism is that it symbolizes our dying and rising with Christ. These are church traditions that take the original word *baptizo* ("to immerse") literally. Those who baptize infants through sprinkling see the act as a sign of the new covenant in the same way circumcision is a sign of the old covenant (Genesis 17:9-14). We can see that a church's belief about baptism's meaning is connected to mode (how we baptize), and its mode is connected to who it believes are baptism's proper subjects (who we baptize). What evangelicals believe is: (1) it is mandated by Christ, (2) it identifies us with Christ and His people in some way, and (3) it is not equivalent to conversion. In the end, all evangelicals emphasize the personal experience of conversion, regardless of baptismal practice (Acts 2:37-38). But baptism's centrality is without question. As we saw in chapter four, Jesus Himself submitted to baptism. Therefore, we baptize.

"Teaching Them to Observe"

Those with backgrounds in education are familiar with terms like pedagogy or didactic. These actually are both connected to New Testament language related to young children and instruction. Discipleship is facilitated by sound instruction. As mentioned in the introduction, "doctrine" simply means "teaching." Reading and studying this book, then, is an exercise designed to teach one to observe Christ's doctrine. "Observe" means to obey. Knowledge, love, and obedience are all bound together in the biblical worldview. This phrase is very important because it links instruction with learning and learning with obedience. This is, after all, evidence of our love for God (John 14:15). Yet there is another important side to this phrase—"all things." As we saw in chapter one, all Scripture is inspired. Therefore, it is useful and profitable in the Christian life. Thus, we must be cautious about privileging certain parts at the expense of others.

"I Am with You"

One of the operations of the Holy Spirit is that of abiding *presence* (chapter five). "Him dwelling with us" means that God is literally with us, granting us power and helping us to embrace His promises throughout the Christian life. This not only begins with conversion (chapter six) and develops in sanctification (chapter six), it continues throughout the church's life as she ministers and fulfills Christ's mission. The Holy Spirit is who empowers Christians to minister in the first place. Whatever else one might say concerning the ministries of the local church, the present empowerment of God is what is essential for true success.

"End of the Age"

Jesus suggests here that His presence abides with the church until the end of the age. This most likely means the end of this earthly age or era (see chapter twelve). While we may differ about the details of the end, the coming of Christ, or life in the age to come, what is certain is that the church must find balance in its mission. Because the scope of God's mission for His church is global, and because apart from Christ's return, there are no perfect Christians, we have no reason to think that our work will be complete before then. "I am with you" demonstrates we can stand firm, diligent, and confident. The phrase "end of the age" signals that there is no excuse for laziness or frivolity. Christ took His mission so seriously that He was willing to die for it. The early apostles were as well, and so should we.

The Shape of Discipleship

The ministry of the church is what enables the church to carry out the mission of Christ in the world. God's people—the church—gather within the four walls of a building week after week. But what should they do? What does a healthy church look like? How does the local church ministry fuel the mission? We begin by exploring one of our metaphors from chapter eight—the body of Christ—and then consider its various practices.

Members of One Body

In several of the New Testament epistles, the human body is used to illustrate what the church is like (Romans 12:3-8; 1 Corinthians 12–14; Ephesians 2–4). The body is healthy when it is: (1) attached to the head (Ephesians 1:22; 4:15), and (2) its various members fulfill their purpose (Ephesians. 4:16). In the same instance both unity and diversity are stressed. Christ's blood is what unites us when we are divided due to selfish desires and misguided aims. The Spirit then creates a community of people united in truth, love, and holiness. It is only then that they can perform meaningful ministry to one another, and also have something to offer the world.

The means given to Christians to edify one another are spiritual gifts. As mentioned in chapter seven, spiritual gifts are those described as given by God to Christians for the mutual edification of the entire church. They differ in number, function, and appearance, yet they are all manifestations of the Spirit "for the common good" (1 Corinthians 12:7). This is another area where some evangelical traditions will differ in terms of which gifts are operative in the church today. What isn't disputable is that every Christian's gift(s) has its place and must be used in harmony with others if the body is to be healthy.

It is at this point that our reflection on ministry should cause us to answer the often-asked question, "Why does God want me to be a church member?" First, the answer is because God has called us to minister to others. How can we do this if we haven't committed ourselves to a local body of believers? Second, how will we be able to fulfill the Great Commission if we aren't taught and equipped? This is why God gave the church teachers in the first place. Third, as we learned in chapter seven, spiritual growth doesn't happen in a vacuum; it happens in a community, a certain kind of environment suitable for growth. As we further consider the practices of the church, we will understand how these relate, and especially what creates a healthy environment primed to foster growth.

Worship

Worship, broadly speaking, has to do with all of life before God. Our ethics or morals can never be thought of separately from our worship. This is what Paul means when he urges the Roman Christians to offer their bodies as living sacrifices unto God (Romans 12:1-2). Everything we do matters to Him! But in a more narrow sense, worship is the specific practice that the Bible describes the early Christian churches performing when they gathered. The biblical testimony can mostly be summarized using Mark Dever's helpful rubric: Read the Bible

(1 Timothy 4:13), Preach the Bible (2 Timothy 4:2), Pray the Bible (1 Timothy 2:1; Matthew 21:13), Sing the Bible (Colossians 3:16), and See the Bible (Luke 22:19).[1] Most churches also see the collection of an offering as an expression of worship (1 Corinthians 16:1-4).

Many church worship services include these elements, but they sometimes err in several ways. Some add extra elements foreign to Scripture. Others don't allow Scripture to be the content of these practices. Others minimize or ignore entire elements called for by Scripture. These problems can be remedied by sticking to the elements taught in Scripture. Beyond this, wisdom must be exercised to determine the appropriate form and circumstances that accompany these elements. After all, many pastors preach biblical sermons, but they differ in length and when they occur in a service. Many churches may sing hymns with biblical content, but they aren't all the same style nor do the same instruments accompany them. However, while Scripture doesn't answer every specific question we may ask, it gives us wisdom and calls for godly leaders to help navigate these issues.

Ordinances

Baptism has always been considered a sacrament or ordinance in evangelical worship. The Lord's Supper is also one that, despite the diversity of opinion concerning its meaning, has been central to Christian worship. Other traditions include foot washing (John 13), anointing of the sick with oil (James 5:14-15), and more. In truth, there are many evangelical practices that have been historically associated with worship, though they differ in their meaning and frequency. In many cases it isn't that we disagree on the validity of the practice, but how we understand its meaning, which, in turn, dictates how frequently and in what setting they are practiced. Ordinances, however, are how we see the Word of Christ in the context of worship.

Fellowship

Acts 2:42-47 presents an attractive picture of what it means for a church to have fellowship. While the early church certainly had its challenges, it also exemplified unity. Christ's death enables us to reconcile to God and to our fellow man. So despite the many differences in the church, the Spirit produces a spirit of fellowship in which the Word, material goods, and joy are generously shared. Fellowship is frequently linked with meals in Scripture, which is why many meals enjoyed by Christians are referred to as times of fellowship. While worship and fellowship are distinct notions, they are related because our commitment to and unity with others honors Him.

Evangelism and Missions

Much has been said already about the centrality of sharing the Gospel, but it is helpful to consider the terms. Evangelism is usually a more limited term referring to the sharing of the Gospel, while missions are related to efforts abroad that are supported by local churches. One might wonder why this even bears mention in relation to worship. John Piper captures it nicely when he says, "Missions exist because worship doesn't."[2] In taking the Gospel to the nations, we hope that many will be converted and begin to worship the true and living God.

Other Practices of the Church

Certainly there are more practices of the church that are biblical. Stewardship is a concept that includes not only the way Christians financially give to the church, but also the way they manage all of their gifts, talents, families, and energies. Discipline is another important dimension of the church's life (see chapter seven). It is intended to be both formative and corrective. On the one hand, it includes many regular church practices—especially teaching—that positively instruct us how to follow Christ. On the other hand, it has a corrective function because wayward church members will sometimes need a personal rebuke in order to cause them to repent and then be restored in their fellowship. The well-being of the church, especially in the context of discipline, has been especially entrusted to leaders. What does the Bible say about church leadership?

The Leadership of the Church

As we saw in the Great Commission, all authority granted to the church comes from God. Yet in His wisdom, He has ordained that His church would have a form of governance designed to shepherd His own flock. In fact, the image of a shepherd is most frequently used to describe the role of a pastor.

Pastors

The word for pastor is often translated as "shepherd" in the New Testament. Most evangelicals also think the language of "elders," "bishops," or "overseers" refers to the same office, usually emphasizing different functions. Robert Picirilli summarizes the pastor's role as a three-fold office: teacher, leader, and shepherd.[3] Preaching is obviously the most visible, regular function that most pastors will fulfill. The ministry of the Word was central to the church's worship, and so a pastor's preaching is a key consideration. It isn't enough, though, to focus on these roles and consider their meaning. First Timothy 3:1-7 also reveals a high moral standard to which aspiring elders and those already serving are held. Hebrews 13:17 also emphasizes their accountability to God as the grounds for their flocks' obedience to their leadership.

Deacons

Early on, God saw fit to lead the church to establish the office of deacon, which simply means "servant" (Acts 6:1-6). After discussing the requirements of a pastor, 1 Timothy 3:8-13 provide some requirements for deacons. The primary distinction is that deacons are servants who are not required to have the gift of teaching, though in some cases they might. Ministering to the needy, especially orphans and widows, was a specific function deacons frequently carried out in Scripture. Traditionally, they have also served the church in other ways, including assisting the pastor in leadership.

The Priesthood of All Believers

It is certainly clear from the Bible that the church's health is tied to the integrity of its leadership. At the same time, we have considered the Scripture's emphasis on "every-member ministry." Every Christian has gifts that should be faithfully used to serve one another. Ephesians 4:11-16 helpfully demonstrates how those in teaching and leadership positions equip others in the church. Likewise, they are edified by the gifts of others. This is related to what Protestant Christians have often called the *priesthood of all believers*. This means we have access to God apart from a human mediator. While pastors have their proper purpose, they are neither the gatekeepers to God or spirituality.

Conclusion

An institution as unique as the church, when it functions properly, becomes its own counterculture in a dark and corrupt world. A culture is a combination of ideas, beliefs, practices, habits, attitudes, and artifacts that define a people. Typically these people exist in some community and have a label they have adopted for themselves. Yet the early Christians did not call themselves "Christians"; they were simply following "the way, and the truth, and the life" (John 14:6). They were eventually called "Christians" (Acts 11:26) — "little Christs." They were certainly present in the world, while also being different and unique. They grew like wildfire in spite of persecution because they were a people on a mission with God. Their minds were set on things above, the things of heaven (Colossians 3:1).

For Further Reading:

Carson, D. A. *The Cross and Christian Ministry: Leadership Lessons from 1 Corinthians.* Grand Rapids, MI: Baker Books, 2004. **(B)**

Horton, Michael S. *A Better Way: Rediscovering the Drama of Christ-Centered Worship.* Grand Rapids, MI: Baker Books, 2002. **(I)**

Leeman, Jonathan. *Church Discipline: How the Church Protects the Name of Jesus.* Wheaton, IL: Crossway, 2012. **(B)**

Marshall, Colin, and Tony Payne. *The Trellis and the Vine: The Ministry Mind-Shift that Changes Everything.* Kingsford, NSW, Australia: Matthias Media, 2009. **(B)**

Pinson, J. Matthew, ed. *Perspectives on Christian Worship: Five Views.* Nashville, TN: B&H Academic, 2010. **(I)**

---

[1] Mark Dever, *The Deliberate Church: Building Your Ministry on the Gospel* (Wheaton, IL: Crossway, 2005), 81-86.

[2] John Piper, *Let the Nations be Glad! The Supremacy of God in Missions* (Grand Rapids, MI: Baker, 1993), 17.

[3] Robert E. Picirilli, *Teacher, Leader, Shepherd: The New Testament Pastor* (Nashville, TN: Randall House, 2007).

10
Angels and Demons

There is likely no trinket more loveable to decorate with than angels. Angels adorn Christmas trees, dashboards, and even commonly appear on jewelry. They occupy a place of sentimental delight in our society. However, for all of our fascination with angels, what does Scripture say? In this chapter, we will consider the doctrine of angels. This will also allow us to consider the biblical teachings about demons as well. Before proceeding, it is important to answer the question about why such a chapter appears in a book on basic Christian doctrine. Few sermons and lessons are given on them. Seemingly, angels have very little to do with the core of Christian thought. However, one theologian helpfully anticipates such misconceptions and explains that "the doctrine of angels is directly and significantly related to most of the major doctrines treated in Christian theology."[1] Angels are related to our views of creation and providence since they were created by God and partly administer His work in the world. They are connected with the doctrine of revelation because they frequently serve as messengers of God. They are even related to the doctrine of man (anthropology) and salvation (soteriology).[2] Therefore, there is good warrant for considering the biblical doctrine on angels and demons.

God's Messengers

Angels, by their very definition, are God's messengers. This is the way the original Greek word can be translated in English. However, in order to understand their role as His messengers or servants, one must consider their origins, characteristics, and ministry that make angels what they are.

Origin

While the creation account in Genesis 1–2 does not specifically describe the creation of angels, it must have occurred sometime after the first day. This is certain because God existed in the beginning as Father, Son, and Spirit, and by Him, all things came into being. The Colossian church had difficulty understanding the proper place of angels in their worship and theology, so the Apostle Paul taught that Christ was supreme not only in redemption, but also in creation:

> For by him all things were created, in heaven and on earth, visible and invisible, whether thrones or dominions or rulers or authorities—all things were created through him and for him.

(Colossians 1:16)

This is such a critical point that John and Hebrews also offer the right perspective on angelic origin. John 1:1-3 says that the Word (Christ) created "all things." In Hebrews, the author emphasizes Christ's supremacy by asserting that He has been given a more excellent name than angels, that He enjoys a unique relationship to the Father, and that He is the object of their worship (Hebrews 1:4-12). In contrast, the angels were created beings designed for worship, praise, and service to God. Nehemiah 9:6 captures it well: "You are the LORD, you alone. You have made heaven, the heaven of heavens, with all their host, the earth and all that is on it, the seas and all that is in them; and you preserve all of them; and the host of heaven worships you."

Characteristics

What are angels like? On the one hand, Scripture describes them as spiritual beings or spirits. This is perhaps why some may doubt their existence, since they cannot be captured on film or studied in a laboratory. On the other hand, they sometimes reveal themselves in bodily form. One of the most notable encounters with angels is Gabriel's appearance to Mary to tell her that she will be the mother of the Messiah (Luke 1:30-31). In other places when angels appear and speak, the Bible presents them as visible, radiant beings. For example, when an angel appeared to the shepherds of Bethlehem upon Jesus' birth, God's glory shone around them (Luke 2:8-9). In Isaiah 6, we see another portrait of angels that reveals them to be majestic creatures. As representatives of God, such characteristics seem to authenticate who they are, who is sending them, and the gravity of their ministry. This calls to mind scenes in which angels execute God's wrath on the wicked, such as slaying Israel's enemies (2 Kings 19:35) or the return of Christ when He comes accompanied by angels (Matthew 24:31).

Another question often asked about angels concerns their number. More specifically, do individual Christians have guardian angels assigned to them? Scripture doesn't directly affirm this, but believers can take comfort in the fact that Scripture often uses the expression "a multitude of the heavenly hosts" to describe the angelic assembly. This seems to suggest that their number is unknown from a human perspective. Suffice to say, there are plenty to laud the name of God and do His bidding! The Bible even uses numerous terms to refer to various types of angelic beings, such as "archangels, "seraphim and cherubim," and even "powers."

Angels are sometimes mysterious to many in modern times, as they were to people in the ancient world. One chief mistake that has been made often is thinking that because angels are spiritual beings, and because God is a spirit, they must be similar in authority, glory, or power. Such an error might lead the church to focus more on angels than on Christ—a problem the early church occasionally made. However, this is an error that Scripture rejects. Hebrews 1 places angels in direct subjection to the will and power of God. Though there was a time when God became flesh and was "a little lower than the heavenly beings" (Psalm 8:5), Christ has returned to the right hand of God and stands "far above all rule and authority and power and dominion" (Ephesians 1:21). This point becomes clearer when we consider the ministry of angels.

Ministry

Psalm 148 is one of many psalms that summons all of creation to worship the living God. It specifically calls angels to praise the Lord (vv. 2, 5). This is because they are servants or ministers of God. As created beings, they are subject to the Lord. They are called "ministers" or "ministering spirits sent out to serve" (Hebrews 1:7, 14). What exactly does this ministry look like?

The first broad aspect of angelic ministry is that of being a *messenger*. In the Old Testament, they fulfilled an important role of giving the law (Deuteronomy 33:2; Galatians 3:19). In the New Testament, they also delivered messages to God's servants (Acts 8:26), expressed God's favor (Luke 1:28) or God's judgment (Acts 12:23), and will one day announce the return of Christ (1 Thessalonians 4:16). Broadly speaking, their ministry is designed to exalt the Lord. This is why angels are frequently pictured as calling the attention of human beings to the Lord, whether it is accepting His Word or rendering proper worship.

The second aspect of angelic ministry has to do with administering care. While they aren't all-powerful beings, they are mighty and use their strength to serve the will of God and the needs of His people. They are shown to "patrol" or oversee human affairs (Zechariah 1:10-11). They are also engaged in ministering to those experiencing spiritual crisis. After being tempted by Satan in the wilderness, Jesus Himself was ministered to by angels (Matthew 4:11). This suggests that God's protection and presence, though mediated by the Holy Spirit, is also a part of the ministry entrusted to His special messengers.

Much more could be said about the biblical significance of angels. However, we cannot adequately consider this without considering their wicked counter-parts—demons. God has His messengers, but Satan has his as well!

Satan's Messengers

C. S. Lewis' *The Screwtape Letters* is perhaps the most intriguing book ever written on the subject of demons. This is because it is both a fictional work, and at the same time reveals deep, biblical reflection on how demons operate in the realm of human affairs. He offers an instructive caution: "There are two equal and opposite errors into which our race can fall about the devils. One is to disbelieve in their existence. The other is to believe, and to feel an excessive and unhealthy interest in them."[3] Christians today should avoid both extremes. Therefore, we will consider the doctrine of *fallen angels* here, and its relevance to trials and temptations.

If we return to angelic origins, we are able to glimpse why demons (or fallen angels) exist in the first place. Genesis doesn't offer the entire picture of this part of Christian doctrine. It simply affirms: (1) God created everything, and (2) angels and demons exist. The first is affirmed quite clearly. The second is seen in the appearance of the serpent in Genesis 3 (whom we later learn to be Satan), as well as appearances of angels elsewhere (Genesis 19:1-2). Evidently the fall of angels occurred sometime between the initial creation and Genesis 3. As Scripture unfolds, only three angels are named specifically: Michael, Gabriel, and Lucifer. The first two are angels who serve God (Daniel 8:16; 10:13). However, the latter one is the most discussed in the Bible.

The Ruler of the Demons

Lucifer is called the "Day Star" (Isaiah 14:12), an anointed guardian cherub (Ezekiel 28:14), and even an angel of light (2 Corinthians 11:14). This initially sounds like another faithful messenger. Yet the biblical message unfolds and shows this to be an angel who once occupied a privileged place among heavenly hosts but rebelled. Along with other angels, he was cast out from the sight of God (Jude 6). This angel, known more commonly as Satan or the devil, now stands in total opposition to the will and Word of God. He is a tempter, a slanderer, and an accuser. He is called the "prince of the power of the air" (Ephesians 2:2), the "prince of demons" (Matthew 12:24), and the "father of lies" (John 8:44), among other deplorable titles. One error Christians make is thinking that because Christ's resurrection sealed Satan's defeat, he is no threat. Indeed, many fallen angels have been bound until the final judgment (1 Corinthians 6:3). Yet many are active in the world, seeking to draw from mankind their own set of "converts." Satan, the chief tempter, has messengers with their own "ministry."

The "Ministry" of Demons: Temptation and Deception

The Apostle Paul warns Christians that their primary oppositions are not visible enemies. It isn't ornery bosses, demanding in-laws, or rising fuel costs. Instead, their primary oppositions are spiritual forces at work in the world (Ephesians 6:10-12). The enemy will not go quietly into the night as the Gospel of Christ spreads and changes hearts and spiritual allegiances. The evil one's fallen angels follow him by promoting false worship and doctrine, blinding people, and empowering false teachers. They tempt believers to turn away from God by causing them to question God's Word and His character. They, at the permission of the sovereign God, are allowed to afflict believers with an eye toward causing them to forsake their Savior (Job 1–2).

Some Christians may fear that this temptation is inescapable. However, the Bible offers us reasons to stand firm. First, we are told that there will always be a way of escape (1 Corinthians 10:13). Second, Christ Himself sympathizes with our weaknesses. Therefore, He is able to help His disciples (Hebrews 2:16-18). Finally, the very nature of the opposition should remind us that demons need not be successful in their interference in our lives. They do have unique strength, and yet they are limited. They are neither all-powerful nor omnipotent (1 Peter 5:8-9). They will not only be completely defeated at the return of Christ, but the call to spiritual warfare and the Holy Spirit's presence shows that we are not up against an unbeatable foe. Satan and his demons are chief among those who oppose the reign of God, but their final fate is sealed.

Conclusion

A number of questions swirl around religious movements associated with spiritism. Entire books have been written on such subjects. However, Peter Schemm offers some of the most concrete biblical counsel for how we ought to view demonic forces in the Christian life. He says that we should be vigilant, give no opportunity or foothold for the devil, actively resist him, and stand firm.[4] When it comes to angels, Christians should not venerate spiritual beings beyond the way Scripture esteems them. Yet we should not be surprised when God's hand intervenes in our lives for both protection and provision. Surely we should be cautious about attributing particular actions directly to angels. However, Christians can walk confidently and engage in spiritual warfare knowing that God has provided the means to overcome such forces. Particularly, He rose from the dead! This changes everything, including our eternal destiny. It is that future we consider in chapters eleven and twelve.

For Further Reading:

Grudem, Wayne. *Systematic Theology: An Introduction to Biblical Doctrine.* Grand Rapids, MI: Zondervan, 2000. **(I)**

Lewis, C. S. *The Screwtape Letters.* San Francisco: HarperCollins, 2001. **(A)**

Moore, Russell D. *Tempted and Tried: Temptation and the Triumph of Christ.* Wheaton, IL: Crossway, 2011. **(B)**

---

[1] Peter Schemm, "The Agents of God: Angels," in *A Theology for the Church,* Daniel L. Akin, ed. (Nashville, TN: B&H Academic, 2007), 293-294.

[2] Ibid.

[3] C. S. Lewis, *The Screwtape Letters* (San Francisco: HarperCollins, 2001), ix.

[4] Schemm, 333-335.

11

Heaven and Hell

W"hat will happen when I die?" This question is inscribed in the heart of every human being. Ideas about heaven certainly flood the consciousness of the broader culture. However, one can attend the occasional funeral and learn that there is something within people's souls that clings to the belief of an afterlife. People refuse to believe that this life is the end. We cannot fathom the idea of nonexistence. It is as if we have been spiritually programmed to look and long for something beyond this mortal life. This is likely what the author of Ecclesiastes intended to convey when he said that God had set eternity into man's heart (Ecclesiastes 3:11).

While many people believe in a pristine place called heaven, fewer believe that someplace like hell exists. When people think of passing through death's chilly waters, they want to know that they and their loved ones have a peaceful existence waiting beyond. Judgment and punishment are unthinkable. However, the biblical story tells of a God who both rewards the righteous and punishes the wicked. Perhaps the greatest reason human beings struggle with this is because our standards for assessing righteousness and wickedness are rather different from God's. We define heaven and hell according to our own preferences, but we also define morality through our own eyes. In this chapter, we will explore the biblical vision of heaven and hell.

Assessing Our Standards

If we were to honestly evaluate ourselves, we would be forced to acknowledge that we often contradict ourselves. We are the types of creatures who will feel wronged if a patrolman tickets us after we've been caught speeding to an important meeting. At the same time, we are outraged by the car that zips past us on the interstate and hope that a police officer catches up to it. We believe in morality, judgment, and fairness—just on our own terms. In truth, all humans long for a world in which justice prevails, but we quickly find this isn't the world in which we live. The existence of heaven and hell help make sense of the justice of God.

People will always assess themselves using their own standards of morality. However, as we saw in chapter two, the Christian God is the One who rules the universe on the basis of His holy standards which reflect His character. He created human beings in His own image, and yet they have turned away from Him. An infinitely righteous and holy God owes such creatures no lenience, no mercy, and surely no grace. However, in Jesus Christ, this same God shows His love, wisdom, and grace by coming to earth, living a sinless life, dying for the sins of many, and rising again in victory over the powers of Satan and hell to offer eternal life to all who trust in Him. It is within this framework that the doctrine of heaven and hell takes shape.

Reward to the Righteous

We begin by considering the "two stages" of the afterlife. While the Old Testament has something to say to Christians about the afterlife, the New Testament offers the clearest insight.

Paradise

The afterlife begins as an intermediate state for both those who have trusted in Christ and those who have rejected Him. One passage that particularly demonstrates this for believers is Luke 23. Two thieves hang on either side of Jesus' cross, but only one saw Jesus for who He was—the Savior. When one thief asked Jesus to remember him when He came into His kingdom, Jesus assured him that he would be with Him in Paradise that very day (Luke 23:43). The significance of this is that it supports Paul's words in 2 Corinthians 5. Human beings can exist, albeit unnaturally, apart from their bodies following death. In Paul's words, for a believer to be absent from the body is to be present with the Lord (2 Corinthians 5:8). As Michael Horton explains, "This intermediate state is God's preservation of the personal consciousness of believers in his presence awaiting the resurrection of the dead."[1]

The Bible uses an array of peaceful, beautiful, and glorious images to describe heavenly life with the Lord. Many times, it is difficult to untangle those passages from the greater glory at the time of Christ's return. Then the realm of heaven will come down to earth. While more on this will be discussed in chapter twelve, for now we will consider what the Bible calls the New Jerusalem.

The New Jerusalem

The scriptural view of the future means an entirely new existence. It does not include souls floating in the clouds, nor some other sentimental portrait. Revelation 21–22, Romans 8, and 2 Peter 3 teach that Christ will ultimately restore the entire creation. As N. T. Wright explains, "Redemption doesn't mean scrapping what's there and starting again from a clean slate, but rather liberating what has come to be enslaved."[2] All of the brokenness that we have known in this life will be renewed and complemented by a new heavenly city coming down to earth—the New Jerusalem. Revelation 21:1-17 portrays it to be great in magnitude, purity, and beauty. Also in its midst is the tree of life and a resplendent river. Eden's glory is regained and even magnified. While heaven is beyond our complete grasp, Scripture offers glimpses and hints of the coming glory.

Life in the new creation is pictured as a time of great blessing for those who labored for Christ. Though there will be no envy or discontentment there, each believer will be rewarded for his or her labors on earth (Ephesians 6:8; Colossians 3:24; James 1:12). This serves as a basis for faithfulness, even in this present life. Christians will still have purpose and tasks in which to engage in the new creation, as they did before the fall. However, it will be sanctified work, free from toil, thorns, and thistles. But the greatest feature of heaven is that it is an unlimited sanctuary filled with God's presence. Revelation 21:22-24 offers one snapshot:

> And I saw no temple in the city, for its temple is the Lord God the Almighty and the Lamb. And the city has no need of sun or moon to shine on it, for the glory of God gives it light, and its lamp is the Lamb. By its light will the nations walk, and the kings of the earth will bring their glory into it.

Ongoing worship is the proper response to such a God. We will never know Him exhaustively, but we will know Him truly. We will endlessly grow in our understanding of God's gracious character (Ephesians 2:6-7). Though this is difficult to understand, married Christians have a foretaste of this. Couples continually grow in their knowledge of their spouse over time. Even men and women who have celebrated 50th anniversaries often remark that they still learn new things about their spouse. If this is true on a human level, how much more of it relates to God!

Randy Alcorn's book, *Heaven,* is a great resource for readers to further pursue this subject. He summarizes the biblical view best:

> When we die, believers in Christ will not go to the Heaven where we'll live forever. Instead, we'll go to an intermediate Heaven. In

that Heaven—where those who died covered by Christ's blood are now—we'll await the time of Christ's return to the earth, our bodily resurrection, the final judgment, and the creation of the new heavens and New Earth. If we fail to grasp this truth, we will fail to understand the biblical doctrine of heaven.[3]

Chapter twelve will further expand the big picture of our future with the Lord, but we must also consider the alternative destiny for unbelievers.

Punishment of the Wicked

As seen in earlier chapters, the human predicament is grave. Those who have not trusted in Christ are, by definition, trusting in something else. The broken relationship between God and man that all human beings inherit at birth remains ruined and tainted because of sin. This condition is so severe that God has ordained a place of eternal judgment, suffering, and sorrow for those who have not turned to Him. Naturally, this provokes many questions and criticisms from those who cannot conceive of a loving God sending people to hell. Here we will consider some of the specific teachings about hell and clarify some misunderstandings.

Sin = Death

God's original warning to human beings was that if they disobeyed Him they would die. Of course, we find that human beings fell into sin and now stand alienated from the God of life. Apart from Him, we face physical and spiritual destruction. Hell is a place in which the realities of death come to fruition in a vivid, conscious, eternal manner. Descriptions such as darkness, weeping, gnashing of teeth, and fiery torment come specifically from the lips of Jesus. He warned that many would profess to know Him, and yet He would tell them to depart from Him because they had trusted in their works and not Him (Matthew 7:21-23).

These descriptions seem to rule out the possibility that this is a temporary judgment. Some who hold to annihilationism argue that unbelievers will either cease to exist at the time of their physical death, or will do so after a period of suffering. However, there is no biblical evidence to support this. This flame is all-consuming. Arguably the most persuasive biblical evidence for the judgment of hell to be ongoing is the story of Lazarus and the rich man in Luke 16. This passage pictures the rich man experiencing judgment after death. He calls out to Lazarus to come from heaven to alleviate his torment. Whether this is taken literally or seen as a parable, even parables are intended to convey the truth! In this case, it won't allow us to soften our perspective on how serious and sorrowful it will be for those apart from Christ. It is said to be "eternal" in countless passages. Some of this judgment is immediate while the rest occurs when the wicked are resurrected bodily (more in chapter twelve). As there are different degrees of reward in heaven, there seem to be varying degrees of punishment in hell (Luke 12:47-48). But it is the fundamental issue of guilt and innocence that many wrestle with.

Innocent or Guilty?

In the Christian worldview, no one is innocent. Everyone apart from Christ stands guilty and condemned before God. Everyone has suppressed the truth and broken God's law (Romans 1–2). The written law only makes sin more apparent because the conscience already convicts the heart of breaking the moral law (Romans 2:12-16; 5:2). However, God lifts condemnation from those incapable of responding to the Gospel, such as infants and the mentally disabled. As Leroy Forlines explains, "The age of accountability is reached when the child has some realization that he or she has sinned against God."[4] Still, all who have received some revelation of God are morally accountable to respond to what they have been given. John 3:16 is a precious verse to many Christians, but John 3:36 is just as important: "Whoever believes in the Son has eternal life; whoever does not obey the Son shall not see life, but the wrath of God remains on him."

Conclusion

The following chapter will continue to explain humanity's future. However, it will focus especially on resurrection and judgment *in light of* Christ's coming kingdom. It is vital to Christian joy and perseverance that they anticipate the glorious place that Christ has prepared for them (John 14:1-4). Those who persevere will be saved and can ultimately look forward to the marriage supper of the Lamb (Revelation 19:6-10). There will be no more husband and wife relationships then (Matthew 22:30), but the union between God and man, and heaven and earth, will be consummated. On the other hand, those whose names are not written in the Lamb's book of life will have no part in such a celebration (Revelation 13:8; 17:8). Because of this, there is a great urgency to the evangelistic task of the church. It isn't simply a matter of adding numbers to a membership roster. Reward and punishment are imperative reminders to Christians to rescue the perishing.

For Further Reading:

Alcorn, Randy. *Heaven.* Carol Stream, IL: Tyndale House Publishers, 2004. **(B)**

Walls, Jerry. *Hell: The Logic of Damnation.* Notre Dame, IN: The University of Notre Dame Press, 1992. **(A)**

Wright, N. T. *Surprised by Hope: Rethinking Heaven, the Resurrection, and the Mission of the Church.* New York: HarperCollins: 2008. **(I)**

---

[1] Michael S. Horton, *The Christian Faith: A Systematic Theology for Pilgrims on the Way* (Grand Rapids, MI: Zondervan, 2011), 912-913.

[2] N. T. Wright, *Surprised by Hope: Rethinking Heaven, the Resurrection, and the Mission of the Church* (New York: HarperCollins: 2008), 96.

[3] Randy Alcorn, *Heaven* (Carol Stream, IL: Tyndale House Publishers, 2004), 42.

[4] F. Leroy Forlines, *The Quest for Truth: Answering Life's Inescapable Questions* (Nashville, TN: Randall House, 2001), 210-212.

12

The Coming Kingdom

Most books on Christian doctrine conclude with a chapter on eschatology, also known as the "study of last things." Christians often have two misconceptions about the end times. First, they tend to reduce this subject to foreboding signs, timeframes, and other speculative guessing that goes beyond the plain teaching of Scripture. Second, they disconnect their reflection on the future from the person and work of Jesus Christ. These are two errors that we will seek to avoid in this chapter. Eschatology is, after all, an immensely important subject since it deals with some of the most profound issues of human existence. It deals with death, judgment, and the return of Christ. It even speaks to the foundation of our hope as Christians. It reminds us that Jesus came into this world preaching the Good News of the *kingdom* of God (Mark 1:14-15). His death and resurrection inaugurated His rule as king. However, it won't be *until He returns* that the kingdom rule of God is completely and entirely implemented on earth as it is in heaven. Until then, our task is to consider what the Bible says about life and death in light of this coming kingdom.

The Last Days?

The New Testament refers to the "last days" on several occasions. While it has been common for some to associate them with a rapture, tribulation period, or another future event, "last days" specifically refers to the time between Christ's first coming and His second coming—regardless of its actual length. It is in these "last days" that God has spoken to us through His Son, whom He appointed the heir of all things (Hebrews 1:1-4). First Corinthians 15:20-28 teaches that all things are subject to the risen Christ. Upon His return, all His enemies will be decisively defeated and abolished, including all authorities and powers—namely death. All must finally proclaim that "Jesus Christ is Lord" to the glory of God the Father (Philippians 2:5-11).

Another way to understand the end is in reference to chapters six and seven. Justification is a definite, once-and-for-all declaration by God that guilty sinners are innocent because of their faith in Jesus Christ. This doesn't rid them from their struggle with sin, but it gains them acceptance before God. It also provides them spiritual resources to contend with sin's power and presence as Christians grow in the grace and knowledge of Jesus Christ. Life in Christ's coming kingdom will mean living under His complete reign as people who are totally conformed to His image. This is what the Bible calls *glorification*. Paul describes this in Philippians 3:20-21: "But our citizenship is in heaven, and from it we await a Savior, the Lord Jesus Christ, who will transform our lowly body to be like his glorious body, by the power that enables him even to subject all things to himself." This coming reality can be best understood when considered in light of the second coming of Christ.

The Return and Reign of Christ

As previously mentioned, eschatological views often say more about dates and times than about Jesus. However, the Bible links the things to come directly with the person and work of Jesus. Specifically, Christ's resurrection and second coming confirm His role as king of creation. Here, some consideration will be given to how this unfolds biblically.

Resurrection

Jesus' resurrection is God's "yes" to His Son's sacrifice. It means that He has accepted that sacrifice to atone for the sins of all who trust in Him by faith. It is also a redemptive act that means that creation has been vindicated. Passages like 1 Corinthians 15 and Colossians 1 point us to the far-reaching implications of Jesus' resurrection. It is the "firstfruits," or the first of other "coming attractions." The raising of His body is the guarantee of future redemption. The earliest Christians believed that Christ's resurrection signaled what God was ultimately going to do for all Christians and the entire creation in the future. However, His return is what finally makes this possible.

Second Coming

When Christ died and rose from the dead, this meant that death no longer would have the final word over those who trust in Christ's death and resurrection *for them*. But the fact that Jesus returned to heaven and left His disciples behind has significant implications for what is to come. He left those disciples with a concrete mission to fulfill—the Great Commission (Matthew 28:18-20).

This call is grounded in the authority that Jesus has been given by the Father Himself—the same authority that 1 Corinthians 15 refers to when it says that He will deliver the kingdom back to the Father after He has destroyed every rule and power. Until that happens, this Commission is binding on every single Christian. Yet it is one that can be embraced with boldness because Christ is with us, even until the end of the age.

While Jesus is present with all believers in some sense now, He is obviously not present physically. Christian hope is founded not on what is unseen, but what we are confident will happen: Christ will return! Though the resurrection initiated the "last days," the second coming will be the centerpiece of the end-times events we often associate with the book of Revelation. However, a survey of evangelical literature reveals that this is an area of wide disagreement. This disagreement relates particularly to the timing of the second coming and the nature of that period of time. A few of these views will be offered here.

The Rapture, the Tribulation, and the Millennium

Though the Bible never actually uses the term "rapture," some Christians believe that it is the time when Christians will be taken out of this world prior to, in the middle of, or following a period of tribulation and persecution. Many differ on whether or not other people can or will be converted during this time. Those who emphasize a tribulation period also point to the New Testament teaching on the antichrist as being a single, great deceiver during this period. The *Left Behind* series of the 1990s perhaps exemplifies the way some understand the symbols, images, and other descriptions in the Bible. On the other hand, some Christians tend to interpret the eschatological language in metaphorical and figurative terms, seeing them as representations of the spiritual realities that will take place.

Another facet of evangelical eschatology pertains to the thousand-year reign, also known as the "millennium." This refers to Revelation 20:1-6, which describes a time when Satan is bound and believers reign with Christ. This is another place where one's hermeneutics will shape what doctrine you ultimately arrive at. Premillennialists say that Christ will return and establish an earthly, thousand-year reign. In the meantime, things will grow worse and worse in the world leading up to this time. Postmillennialism says that Christ will return following a thousand-year reign in which He is *physically* absent. Some adherents of this perspective expect the earth to improve as many are saved and as the church ushers in the kingdom following a period of spiritual revival. Amillennialists do not believe the thousand years of Revelation are literal years. In fact, most believe that Christ's reign is happening now and His second coming will be what inaugurates the final resurrection and judgment. There are even some believers who hold to preterism. This says that "most or all of Christian eschatology was fulfilled in the first century" and "that the tribulation came to pass in the fall of Jerusalem in AD 70."[1] Thankfully, there are numerous books available that survey, explain, and compare these positions for interested readers.

It is appropriate to study such events that we associate with the end times. However, the more urgent concern of Christian eschatology is what Christ's return *means* or *accomplishes*. Christ's return initiates the *eschaton*, or the end— the consummation of all things for which we have hoped. It means the promise of a new and glorious body.

The Promise of the Resurrected Body

There are many myths related to the future existence of Christians. Scripture unwaveringly declares that Christians will one day enjoy resurrected bodies like the one Jesus has. Humans won't become something more or less than human. Some have often misinterpreted Jesus' words in Matthew 22 to mean that Christians will become angels. N. T. Wright ardently argues against this: "Contrary to what people sometimes suggest...he didn't say that in the resurrection God's people would *become* angels; he said that they would in certain respects be *like* angels [Matthew, Mark] or *equal to* angels [Luke]."[2]

For Christians, Christ's resurrection is the "firstfruits," to use Old Testament language. It foreshadowed what was to happen in the future. Even saints before the time of Christ had some sense of this. Job said, "For I know that my Redeemer lives, and at the last he will stand upon the earth. And after my skin has been thus destroyed, yet in my flesh I shall see God" (Job 19:25-26). Then in 1 Corinthians 15, Paul confronts the church with the sharpest argument for why Jesus was serious when He said, "I am the resurrection and the life. Whoever believes in me, though he die, yet shall he live" (John 11:25). The Holy Spirit's presence in believers' lives is a down-payment of a future, miraculous act of raising up bodies. It is with such resurrected bodies that the righteous and the wicked will stand before the Lord and be judged on the final day.

The Promise of Judgment

As we saw in chapter eleven, the corollary of resurrection is judgment (John 5:26-29). Many Christians often diminish the gravity of death since they believe in heaven. But Randy Alcorn helpfully cautions that "we shouldn't glorify or romanticize death–Jesus didn't. He wept over it (John 11:35)."[3] Hebrews 9:27-28 adds further magnitude to the experience of death: "And just as it is appointed for man to die once, and after that comes judgment, so Christ, having been offered once to bear the sins of many, will appear a second time, not to deal with sin but to save those who are eagerly waiting for him." Though both believer and unbeliever go to intermediate states of blessing and punishment, they both are judged in terms of their professions of faith as well as their works. Christians are rewarded in the afterlife, and the wicked are punished accordingly. Regardless of how one interprets the Great White Throne Judgment of Revelation 20, whether or not one's name is in the book of life distinguishes what their destiny is. Though Christians will one day judge the world (1 Corinthians 5), the all-knowing God of heaven is the only one One who has seen every deed, heard every word, and peered into every heart. Those who die apart from Christ are separated from Him, and are eventually cast into the lake of fire (Revelation 20:15). His time of offering people the chance to repent and trust in Him will expire.

Restoration

As we saw in chapter eleven, heaven is just the beginning. The intermediate state is what Christians who die will experience prior to the return of Christ. It is only then that heaven and earth join and we witness the New Jerusalem described in Revelation 20–22. Christians see what God has done in their lives as individuals and know that this foreshadows what "he one day plans to do with the entire universe."[4] Creation will be set free from its bondage to decay, and it will be restored to its former glory (Romans 8:20-21). Most biblical scholars believe it will actually transcend its original beauty and splendor since saints who have endured tribulation and been redeemed will be worshipping God. Either way, the Bible promises both personal blessing ("God will wipe away every tear from their eyes") and cosmic transformation ("Then I saw a new heaven and a new earth"). The lion will lay down with the lamb, and there will be eternal peace (Isaiah 11:6-9; 60:19-22). This is the destiny of the Christian.

A few things are certain that have been points of historical, Christian consensus: (1) Christ will physically return; (2) the righteous and the wicked will have resurrection bodies; (3) every single person will be judged by God; (4) Christians will spend eternity in the new heavens and earth that God establishes; and (5) unbelievers will be forever cast out of God's presence into eternal punishment. Beyond these, there is no room for biblical dialogue and discussion.

Conclusion

We often dislike the idea of things coming to an end, whether it be a beautiful day, an exciting sporting event, or a vacation. However, our lives are filled with endings and beginnings. To a large degree, it is helpful to think of the end times with this perspective. Though our earthly pursuits will end, Christ's return will usher in a brand-new existence that is consistent with God's original intent for humanity. It is no accident that we find a garden in this heavenly city on earth. It is a sign of a new beginning, but a beginning which will have no end.

In the meantime, Jesus has given His people every tool necessary to be prepared. In the words of the Apostle Paul, "Therefore, my beloved brothers, be steadfast, immovable, always abounding in the work of the Lord, knowing that in the Lord your labor is not in vain" (1 Corinthians 15:58). The Great Commission is not only a message of salvation. It is a message that reminds us that the cross means there is hope in this life because Jesus will return and reign. Until then, we are called to pray, "Thy kingdom come. Thy will be done, on earth as it is in heaven."

For Further Reading:

Bock, Darrell, ed. *Three Views on the Millennium and Beyond.* Grand Rapids, MI: Zondervan, 1999. **(I)**

Craft, Jeremy. "Living in Light of the Kingdom: Reframing Our Eschatology." *Helwys Society Form,* June 25, 2012. http://www.helwyssocietyforum.com/?p=2421. **(B)**

Hultberg, Alan, ed. *Three Views on the Rapture: Pretribulation, Prewrath, or Posttribulation.* Grand Rapids, MI: Zondervan, 2010. **(I)**

Ladd, George Eldon. *The Gospel and the Kingdom: Scriptural Studies in the Kingdom of God.* Grand Rapids, MI: Eerdmans, 1990. **(B)**

Walls, Jerry L., ed. *The Oxford Handbook of Eschatology.* New York: Oxford University Press, 2010. **(A)**

---

[1] Russell D. Moore, "Personal and Cosmic Eschatology," in *A Theology for the Church,* Daniel L. Akin, ed. (Nashville, TN: B&H Academic, 2007), 894.

[2] N. T. Wright, *Surprised by Hope: Rethinking Heaven, the Resurrection, and the Mission of the Church* (New York: HarperCollins, 2008), 38.

[3] Randy Alcorn, *Heaven* (Carol Stream, IL: Tyndale House Publishers, 2004), 467.

[4] Moore, 913.

Conclusion

No one sets out to erect a sturdy structure unless he first gives attention to the foundation. In many ways, the foundation of Christian existence is Jesus Christ. Though no one living today has ever walked with Jesus in the same way His disciples did, evangelical Christians believe that the Bible faithfully presents Jesus to us. It is the inspired, infallible, inerrant Word of God. It is God's primary means for revealing Himself to us by presenting us with the truth of God's dealings with His creatures, from Genesis to Revelation. Yet the Bible also provides an overarching account of Christianity. It can be understood using the following six-fold rubric:

Creation – Chaos – Covenant – Cross – Church – Consummation

In creation we see the greatness and glory of God. However, creation gives way to chaos as man and woman doubt and disobey God's words by allowing the tempter to lead them astray. Creation, though God's gift, is warped by sin's entrance into the world. The good news is that from Genesis onward, God shows that He is a promise-making God by the covenants He enacts with people. These covenants culminate in the life of Jesus Christ, whose cross makes possible a new covenant with better promises! As part of this new covenant, the cross opens the door to a glorious institution that Jesus calls the church, or His bride. The church isn't an assembly of perfect people, but they are God's people. They have experienced transformation because of the power of the Holy Spirit in their lives. This church is given a mission—a Great Commission—to take their message to the world. This is currently where things stand for Christians in the world today. They live sometime between "church" and "consummation." However, they are able to endure because they know a day is coming when Christ will return and make all things new. Every hint of sin's power and presence will be removed from their lives. They will inherit new, glorified bodies to inhabit the new heavens and new earth that Christ will bring about.

As mentioned earlier in the book, a great deal more could be said about each doctrine this book surveys. Christians who desire to grow should study the Scriptures more deeply so they can better grasp these teachings. But then they must take that understanding and apply it toward real-life discipleship. Likewise, it is sometimes when Christians participate in the practices and worship of the church (such as singing, serving, listening, and other forms of "doing") that sound doctrine will be taught and reinforced in their minds and hearts. While doctrinal books such as this are essential, the Bible, put into practice in the church and world, is often the best course of instruction one can have. Stanley Hauerwas and William Willimon capture the aim of Scripture well: "The Bible's concern is whether or not we shall be faithful to the gospel, the truth about the way things are now that God is with us through the life, cross, and resurrection of Jesus of Nazareth."[1] In other words, God's truth is not intended merely for information, but for transformation. So as we carefully attend to the biblical beliefs we hold, we should also pay closer attention to our conduct and character. Only in doing this can we obey the most important commandments God ever gave: "Love the Lord your God with all your heart and with all your soul and with all your. strength and with all your mind," and "Love your neighbor as yourself."

[1]Stanley Hauerwas and William H. Willimon, *Resident Aliens* (Nashville, TN: Abingdon Press, 1989), 22.